MW01075149

WISDOM FROM
POPE PAUL VI

Compiled by
Mary Leonora Wilson, FSP

P*auline*
BOOKS & MEDIA

Boston

Library of Congress Control Number: 2018948419

CIP Data is available.

ISBN 10: 0-8198-8377-8

ISBN 13: 978-0-8198-8377-3

Excerpts from Pope Paul VI's magisterium texts copyright © Libreria Editrice Vaticana. Used with permission.

Scripture quotations contained herein are from the *New Revised Standard Version Bible: Catholic Edition,* copyright © 1989, 1993, Division of Christian Education of the National Council of the Churches of Christ in the United States of America. Used by permission. All rights reserved.

Cover design by Rosana Usselmann

Cover art by Amedeo Brogli

Introduction, A Brief Biography, and prayers following the meditations written by Mary Leonora Wilson, FSP

Selected Prayers of Pope Paul VI translated by Mary Leonora Wilson, FSP

All rights reserved. No part of this book may be reproduced or transmitted in any form or by any means, electronic or mechanical, including photocopying, recording, or by any information storage and retrieval system, without permission in writing from the publisher.

"P" and PAULINE are registered trademarks of the Daughters of St. Paul.

Copyright © 2018, Daughters of St. Paul

Published by Pauline Books & Media, 50 Saint Paul's Avenue, Boston, MA 02130–3491

Printed in the U.S.A.

www.pauline.org

Pauline Books & Media is the publishing house of the Daughters of St. Paul, an international congregation of women religious serving the Church with the communications media.

1 2 3 4 5 6 7 8 9   22 21 20 19 18

CONTENTS

INTRODUCTION

"What did you go out to see? A prophet? Yes, I tell you, and more than a prophet."

MT 11:9

What Jesus said to the crowds about John the Baptist rings true twenty centuries later about another who would bear the Italian equivalent of that name: *Giovanni Battista Montini*. The Latins have an expression, *Nomen est omen*, which means "The name is a sign." No wonder that Giovanni Battista Montini, the man we now know as Pope Paul VI, is both a prophet and a saint!

I was thrilled when I heard that Pope Paul VI was going to be canonized; he has been a mentor and model to me for more than fifty years. This mentoring started—even though I wasn't aware of it—when I was just a teenager. I entered the congregation of the Daughters of Saint Paul on June 29, 1963, the same day that Pope Paul VI was crowned. The coronation ceremony was fascinating, but foreign to me. It was like opening a time capsule. Little did I know, I was witnessing the elaborate ceremony for the last time. The coronation was just one of the many trappings of aristocracy that would be removed, prompted by subsequent decisions of Pope Paul VI to simplify the papacy and render it more evangelical.

Paul VI had been elected pope eight days before, thus my entrance into religious life was ushered in with a new Pope. I joined a community whose mission is to use every means of communication available to proclaim Christ from the rooftops and on all the streets and byways of the world—the very mission of the first apostles and disciples! I was filled with the enthusiasm of youth. Every day of convent life was new and exciting, and I had fallen in love with Jesus Christ and his Church. Unconsciously, I was looking for people who could direct me always closer to the Lord. I had no idea that the newly elected pontiff would be one of those people.

Just months after his coronation, Pope Paul VI reconvened the Second Vatican Council. I wasn't yet familiar with Church councils, but in community we followed every session and read every document as it was issued. Not only that, we also published them for everyone else to read. As a community, we subscribed to the weekly English edition of *L'Osservatore Romano*, the Vatican newspaper. We read some articles aloud together, especially the words of the Holy Father. I began to look forward to them even though the ecclesiastical language and sentence structure challenged me. The words of the pope struck a chord in my soul.

In those early days I was especially impressed with his love for Christ and the Church, his insistence on dialogue and ecumenism, his concern about rampant injustice and escalating violence in the world, and his unwavering serenity and gentleness despite harsh public criticism. I was particularly touched by his compassion, fired by his missionary vision, and awed by the way he embraced and carried the Cross of Christ. Pope Paul VI stoked the fire of my own love of Christ. More by his life than by his words, he taught me what it means to be a disciple of the Master. His weekly addresses illuminated my theology studies, and as I studied Scripture I began to recognize that he was indeed a contemporary prophet. He became "my pope."

In the following pages, you will find some of the most moving passages from Pope Paul VI. Each selection ends with a brief prayer to serve as a springboard for your own prayer and reflection. In Pope Saint Paul VI, may you discover a spiritual friend and mentor for your own journey with the Lord, just as I did so many years ago.

MARY LEONORA WILSON, FSP

A Brief Biography

Battista Montini

Pope Saint Paul VI was born on September 26, 1897, at Concesio, near Brescia, in the Lombardy region of northern Italy. He was baptized on September 30 and given the name Giovanni Battista Montini—actually, Giovanni Battista Enrico Antonio Maria Montini!

Battista was the second son of Giorgio Montini and Giuditta Alghisi. His father was a non-practicing lawyer and landowner, the editor of the local Catholic newspaper, and a parliamentary deputy. Battista's mother, although orphaned as a child, was from a noble family and schooled in a French-speaking convent in Milan. She would become the leader of the Catholic Women of Brescia. Battista was one of three children, all boys. His older brother, Lodovico, was born just one year before, and his younger brother, Francesco, three years after.

In 1903, at the age of six, Battista began to attend a Jesuit school. The Montini boys were steered in the family tradition of medicine and public service, but Battista dreamed of becoming a writer. Because literature was encouraged in the Montini household, Battista was familiar with all the great European classics. He was also greatly influenced by his father's editorial work.

Battista became a passionate bicyclist, but as he grew into a teenager he recognized he would never be a sportsman. One day, while cycling with his brother Lodovico, he suffered what appeared to be a stroke and was diagnosed as a "serious cardiac imbalance." Heart problems remained with him for the rest of his life, making any strenuous exercise unthinkable.

In fact, when Battista was seventeen years old, he had to leave his Jesuit school and finish his studies privately because of his health. This also meant leaving his best friend, Andrea Trebeschi. The parting was difficult. Andrea invited Battista to write a page in his diary. In that entry Battista expressed his desire to become a priest.

While his desire was not a total surprise, neither was it expected. Although Battista was Jesuit educated, spiritually he was very much influenced by the Oratorians, who ran his home parish: Sant'Antonio de la Pace. He was attracted by their freedom of spirit. The pastor, Father Giulio Bevilacqua, was a lifelong friend and mentor; and the assistant pastor, Father Paolo Caresana, became his confessor and spiritual director from the time Battista was a teenager until the priest died in 1973.

From the Priesthood . . .

As he pondered and prayed over his vocation, Battista's first desire was to become a Benedictine monk. But the monks dissuaded him because he didn't have the health to cope with the demands of monastic life. It was a huge disappointment for Battista. He continued to wrestle with his vocation, trying to understand where God was calling him. He decided to be a diocesan priest. In 1915 Italy entered World War I. Battista was rejected for military service because of his health.

A year later he was accepted into the seminary, only to find out that there would be only two seminarians instead of five because every other candidate had been conscripted! Thus, Battista became an "external student," living and studying at home while attending twenty lectures per week. Classes were held in the monastery of the Church of the Most Holy Body of Christ in Brescia, since the seminary building was being used as a warehouse for a military hospital. In those lonely and confusing years, his spiritual director, Father Caresana, helped him see his way through. "His fatherhood was my seminary," Battista would later attest.

The war ended on November 11, 1918. Post-war reconstruction began and Battista's preparation for the priesthood intensified. He was ordained on May 29, 1920, at the age of twenty-two. The white chasuble he wore was made from his mother's wedding dress.

Once again, health was a deciding factor for Montini's future. His bishop, unwilling to "ordain him for paradise," decided not to risk his precarious health in a country parish, but sent him to Rome to study for a doctorate in history.

. . . To the Vatican

As the saying goes, "Man proposes but God disposes." After barely one year at the Lombardy college of Rome, Father Montini was summoned by Bishop Pizzardo who told him that he was to enter the Academy for Noble Ecclesiastics, the school for Vatican diplomats. Father Montini was not terribly happy. He neither sought nor wanted a diplomatic career. He felt trapped. The canonical approach to life was not his, but he turned his mind from philosophy, history, and literature to study canon law with the Jesuits at the Gregorian. He had the heart of a monk and mistrusted the academy, where so many students took a path of ambition and honors. But the wheels of destiny had begun to turn and would not be stopped. God himself was conducting the train that would take Father Montini to the halls of the Vatican.

On January 22, 1922, Pope Benedict XV died. Two weeks later, on February 6, Pope Pius XI was elected.

All was not well in Italy. Mussolini was preparing to march on Rome. The Church's main task was to cope with the fascist regime during that dangerous time. Bishop Pizzardo sent the young Father Montini to Milan to finish his studies "as soon as possible." In December 1922 he was awarded his doctorate and sent back in Rome, where another surprise awaited him: Father Battista Montini was to enter the service of the Secretariat of State.

After a four-month stint working for the papal nuncio in Poland, at the age of twenty-six he began his Roman apprenticeship in the Secretariat. He spent the next thirty-two years of his life there. The Holy Father named him chaplain to the Catholic students of Rome. In the morning he dealt with issues between the Vatican and the Italian government; in the afternoon he sought to deepen the spiritual, intellectual, and liturgical life of his students.

Father Montini's work with the students made him especially hated by members of the fascist party. In 1925, all political parties had been dissolved—except the fascists. Under fascist rule, all democratic associations were outlawed, people were arrested and deported without trial, and Catholic students were being brutally assaulted by fascist gangs. At this time Father Montini was in charge of the Catholic student movement throughout the entire country, putting him in the front line of battle as the leader of the intellectual opposition. Mussolini denounced Father Montini to Pope Pius XI for allowing lay groups such as Catholic Action* to be used for

---

* Founded in Europe in 1867 and still active today, Catholic Action is an association of Catholics that strives to uphold and defend Christian values inspired by the teachings of the Roman Catholic Church.

political ends. The regime methodically broke up student congresses, banned the newspaper edited by Montini's father and destroyed the presses.

Father Montini did not back down. He founded *La Sapienza*, a weekly newspaper to develop a militantly Catholic intellectual elite and personally contributed many articles to it. With a friend he founded a small publishing house named *Studium* that put out a monthly intellectual review of the same name. Montini was the editor and chief contributor.

Attacks on Catholic Action intensified. In the spring of 1931 all Catholic congresses were canceled, all Catholic youth movements dissolved, properties confiscated, and members violently attacked. Public meetings were permanently suspended, forcing the organization to go underground.

It has been reported that when Mussolini visited the Vatican in 1932, he let the pope know that relations between Italy and the Holy See would improve only if Montini were forbidden contact with student groups. Without warning, Father Montini was thanked and dismissed from his post as national chaplain of the Catholic Students. He had been sacrificed to placate the storm. He submitted, accepting it as the Divine Will. But Father Battista Montini was a creative thinker. "Learning—for life" was his motto. Granted, it was a moment of crisis, but he would not waste time brooding. Later that year, he collaborated in founding a new movement of university graduates, the *Movimento Laureati Cattolici*. It would become instrumental in the formation of those who would eventually lead the Christian Democratic Party after the collapse of fascism.

At this time Father Montini was appointed the assistant to Cardinal Eugenio Pacelli, the then Secretary of State, soon to be elected Pope.

In a World at War

Europe was bracing for a second World War. Mussolini and Hitler became allies. As tension mounted Pope Pius XI died, and on March 2, 1939, white smoke signaled a new pontiff—Pope Pius XII.

On September 1 of the same year, Germany invaded Poland and the Second World War began. During the war Pope Pius XII entrusted Father Montini with the organization and direction of the Holy See's relief work. Father Montini hid political refugees and Jews in convents, seminaries, schools, and parishes, helping them with means of escape. In 1944 alone, he organized the distribution of almost two million portions of free food. The Papal Residence of Castel Gandolfo and Vatican City were open to refugees. Father Montini's efforts saved an estimated 860,000 people. Protection was also provided to hundreds of Allied soldiers who had escaped from Axis prison camps. At the pope's request Montini created an information office researching the whereabouts of POW's and refugees. From 1939–1947 the office received almost ten million requests and sent out eleven million replies.

The war brought great suffering to Montini: his parents died, the Germans occupied his parental home, his brother Francesco fought in the Resistance, and his boyhood friend, Andrea, died in the concentration camp of Guthausen.

The war ended in Europe on May 8, 1945, with the unconditional surrender of the Axis powers. By this time, Montini, who was now a monsignor, was the most important person in the Vatican after the pope. The moment peace was declared, Montini set about post-war reconstruction.

Battista Montini worked in the service of the Church in the Secretariat of State from 1922 to 1954; however, a new chapter of his life was about to begin.

From Secretary to Shepherd

It was December 1954. Cardinal Schuster, the archbishop of Milan had just died. From his own sickbed, the ailing Pope Pius XII appointed Monsignor Montini to head the diocese "as his personal gift to Milan." Nine days later, on December 12, Montini was consecrated bishop.

Milan, called the "secular city," was a notable communist stronghold and would require a courageous and diplomatic leader. Although he had never even been a pastor or an assistant pastor, Montini was to be that leader. He set out with trepidation and trust—trust in the one Shepherd and Master, choosing as his motto: "*In nomine Domini*" (In the name of the Lord).

Bishop Montini was noted for being a friend of the working class and the poor. He went into the mines, toured factories, mingled with workers (at times, amid jeers), visited communist districts, and visited the sick in their homes. He founded a priestly association called Missionaries of the World of Work. But not everyone appreciated his efforts. One year after his arrival, a bomb was thrown into his residence.

Still, Bishop Montini persevered. Many Milan churches had been bombed during the war, so he became a builder of churches—close to one hundred of them. But he also built the Church from within by reforming pastoral care, seeking to win workers back to the Catholic Church, and creating new parishes. He also constructed schools, dispensaries, and community centers in poor districts; provided housing for the poor; and established the Office of Charity to provide free medical and legal advice.

When Pope Pius XII was succeeded by Pope John XXIII, Montini was his first cardinal. Pope John XXIII appointed him simultaneously to several Vatican congregations. Then the Holy Father did something completely unexpected. On January 25, 1959, he called the Second Vatican Council! The Spirit blows where he wills, but doesn't always let everyone in on his plans. Cardinal Montini was just as surprised as everyone else. However, the pope who began the council would not bring it to conclusion. After only one session of the Second Vatican Council, Pope John XXIII died on June 3, 1963.

Habemus Papam! We Have a Pope!

On June 21, 1963, Cardinal Montini was elected pope and chose the name Paul VI. Reflecting on this election, he wrote:

> Perhaps the Lord has called me to this service not because I have any aptitude for it, not so much that I can govern the Church in its present difficulties, but so that I may suffer something and thus that it may be clear that it is the Lord, and no one else, who guides and saves it.

He chose as his namesake the great Apostle Paul, indicating that the life and teachings of the Apostle would set the tone for his pontificate—as it certainly did!

Pope Paul VI reconvened the Council on September 29, 1963, and brought it to completion on the feast of the Immaculate Conception, December 8, 1965. Four key priorities marked these Council sessions: a deepened understanding of the Church, internal church reforms, ecumenism—advancing the unity of Christians, and dialogue with the world.

In *Lumen Gentium,* the council reminds the faithful that the universal call to holiness, asked for by Our Lord himself (see Mt 5:48), is the ultimate purpose of the council's teachings. At the close of the council, the Holy Father proclaimed Mary, the Mother of the Church.

Like so many popes before him and after him, this pope was especially devoted to Our Lady. His personal secretary told a story that when Paul VI was visiting the Philippines, on his arrival at the airport, he was attacked by a deranged man with a knife. The knife pierced the flesh, but the wound was not serious, or so the pope said. He continued the tour as planned, keeping everything well hidden under his red cape. It was only when he was back in the rooms where they were staying that he let someone care for the wound. Then it was discovered that a large Miraculous Medal worn by the Holy Father had been visibly dented by the attacker's knife, deflecting the knife and minimizing the injury. Later on, speaking to the same secretary, the pontiff asked, "Do you wear a Miraculous Medal?" When the secretary said yes, the Pope added, "Make sure it is a big one!"

Paul VI made several other international trips. When we think of popes who traveled the world, we especially think of Pope John Paul II. However, the first "Pilgrim Pope" was Paul VI. He was the first pope to fly in a plane; the first to travel to the Near East; to visit Israel and India; to set foot in the United Nations; and to visit Colombia, Uganda, the Philippines, and Australia. Peter in the person of Paul was once again traveling the world as a missionary, evangelizing with word and example. These missionary trips of Paul VI opened the way for the universal travel of future popes.

Pope Paul VI had a real concern for the poor. Even before becoming pope he was known to give away his own money and belongings to those who needed them more. He would even forget his own needs—more than once it happened that he was left without bus fare to get back home. As a monsignor, working in the Secretariat of State, he gave away his bedding to a poor woman for her children. As pope, he used a simple bishop's mitre and sold the jewel-laden, three-tiered papal tiara, and gave the money to the poor. His own apartment was simply furnished. He wore a simple cope instead of the large, decorative papal mantum (cloak), and abolished the pontifical court. He reached out to orphans, prisoners, and the sick—helping wherever he could.

It's said that when he was a cardinal, each week on Friday (the day when the Church commemorates the crucifixion of Jesus Christ) precisely at 3:00 PM, the Archbishop used to disappear from his house. Nobody knew where he went except the secretary who accompanied him. He would seek out some sick person, whether in the slums of the outlying districts or in some poor shack. His secretary would see him kneel by the bedside of the sufferer and attend to his or her needs. When the young priest reappeared to tell him that it was time to go, he would find the archbishop intent on serving the patient like a nurse or an affectionate and efficient relative.

Pope Paul VI is famous for his 1968 encyclical letter, *Humanae Vitae*. By all standards this letter is prophetic. In upholding the sacredness of human life, the dignity of married love, the purpose of marriage, and the primacy of God in the act of procreation, Pope Paul VI took a bold and courageous stand. He defined these as absolutes on which the Church cannot yield. The pope did not hesitate to look beyond the present and clearly point out where a contraceptive mentality would lead. He warned the faithful and the world of the "grave consequences that follow," such as conjugal infidelity and the destruction of families, the general lowering of morality and related social ills, loss of respect for woman, reducing her to a mere object for the selfish enjoyment of man's desires, loss of reverence for life, for human sexuality, for God's plan. It is enough to reflect on the evolution of society and its laws since *Humanae Vitae*, to recognize that he was right. It is hardly surprising that both miracles for the beatification and the canonization of Pope Saint Paul VI were cures of babies in the womb—the stamp of God's approval on the teaching of a courageous pope!

The storm of protest and criticism that followed the encyclical became a dark and painful night for the Holy Father. Referring to it, he said, "Now I understand Saint Peter: he came to Rome twice—the second time to be crucified." Yet this encyclical, together with *Populorum Progressio*, promulgated one year prior, are considered the glory of Paul VI's pontificate.

Populorum Progressio (*On the Development of Peoples*), is an eloquent plea for the equal distribution of goods and covers free trade, the nobility of work, population growth, racism, nationalism, capitalism, dialogue between nations, and even immigration. It's a well-developed compendium of the Church's social teachings and reflects the Holy Father's concern for the poor and the worker.

Other notable documents of Pope Paul VI's pontificate include *Evangelii Nuntiandi* (*On Evangelization in the*

Modern World), which Pope Francis called "the greatest pastoral document written to date"; *Gaudete in Domino* (*On Christian Joy*); and *Marialis Cultus* (*On Marian Devotion*).

Among his many other achievements, he published the New Roman Missal and the new Breviary; he enlarged and internationalized the Sacred College, giving many countries their first Cardinal; he reorganized the Curia. He proclaimed Saint Teresa of Ávila and Saint Catherine of Siena as Doctors of the Church, opening the way for other holy women to receive this title. And he instituted World Communications Day, proclaimed the Year of Faith in 1967, the Creed of the People of God, as well as the Holy Year in 1975.

Pope Saint Paul VI was a man whose heart beat in unison with humanity. He was deeply moved by the spiritual needs of humanity and sought to respond. His analysis of the present and anticipation of the future was discerning, prayerful, and prophetic. His friendships were true and deep, his faith trusting and serene. Despite his introverted nature, he had the courage that is typical of the saints. He was a man of God.

The Last Pilgrimage

But the life of this man of God was never easy and remained marked with the sign of the cross until the end. If the cross is the sign of God's intimacy and friendship, then the Lord was most intimate with Pope Paul VI. On March 16, 1978, Aldo Moro, a prominent statesman, twice Prime

Minister of Italy, leader of the Christian Democratic Party, and lifelong friend of Pope Paul VI was kidnapped by the Red Brigade, a left-wing terrorist group. Fifty-five days later he was murdered. Those fifty-five days and nights were sheer agony for the Holy Father. In a last, but futile, attempt to save him, the eighty-year-old pontiff wrote a personal letter to Moro's kidnappers. The pope's plea went unheeded. Moro's death was the last nail of Pope Paul VI's own crucifixion. He died three months later.

On June 29, 1978, the fifteenth anniversary of his coronation, he examined his fidelity to God and to the Church and said farewell.

His last audience, August 2, 1978, was on Christian joy.

The next three days he suffered from an acute fever, falling into a deep sleep on Sunday, August 6, the feast of the Transfiguration. At 6:00 PM, Mass was celebrated next to his bedroom and he received Holy Communion. After Mass, the pope was heard softly repeating the Our Father. He lingered for another three hours while those around him offered the prayers for the dying. At 9:41 pm, in the glow of the feast of the Transfiguration, Pope Paul VI passed to eternal life.

He had asked for a simple funeral and to be "buried in the earth with a simple stone to indicate the place. . . . I do not desire any special tomb, just some prayers to obtain God's mercy."

FAITH

"It is Jesus Christ I preach day in and day out. His name I would see echo and reecho for all time even to the ends of the earth!"

Life Is You, O God!

"Blessed are you, O LORD, the God of our ancestor Israel, forever and ever. Yours, O LORD, are the greatness, the power, the glory, the victory, and the majesty; for all that is in the heavens and on the earth is yours; yours is the kingdom, O LORD, and you are exalted as head above all. Riches and honor come from you, and you rule over all. In your hand are power and might; and it is in your hand to make great and to give strength to all. And now, our God, we give thanks to you and praise your glorious name."

1 CHR 29:10–13

O God, under every aspect you are necessary. Today you belong to us, O unrivalled God, God of mystery, of peace, and of beatitude.

We confess this: we have bent our heads senseless with pride, with self-sufficiency and foolishness, and before the exigencies of God's kingdom we have regenerated our consciences in the sincerity and wisdom of humility. . . .

Faith is Life. It is Life because it reaches you, O Lord—even though only on the limiting shore of our capacity to know and love you—you who are the ocean of Being; the surpassing and incumbent fullness of all Existence; the heaven of the unfathomable depths, not only of the earth and of the cosmos, but equal only to yourself, infinite beyond space; Father of everything that exists. Life is you, O God, suspended as a beatifying lamp cast upon the shadow of our stuttering experience, in contact with the world, with history, with our own mysterious interior solitude. The more vast and unknown the panorama that science and civilization opens up to our eager and ever shortsighted gaze, so much the more do we need your sovereign light. And this too will remain. We shall draw from faith, of which Christ, the Father's Word, is the source, that extra light which human knowledge needs to advance freely and faithfully on its continuing path, glad to be able to alternate rational and experimental study with prayer. Yes, this is the exclamation, this is the song of the soul that confirms these principles and integrates and sublimates them. . . .

The wisdom of fraternal love, which with strength and works that are rightly called Christian, has characterized the history of the holy Church, will explode with new fruitfulness, with victorious happiness, with regenerating social consciousness. Not hatred, not strife, not avarice, will be its dialectic, but love—the love that generates love, the love of man for man: for you, O Christ, discovered in the suffering and in the need of each of man and woman. . . .

In this way let our journey begin again, in courage and in joy, through time toward the last encounter, which even now puts on our lips the final invocation: "Come, Lord Jesus!" (Rev 22:20)

GENERAL AUDIENCE, DECEMBER 24, 1975

The beauty of creation and the goodness that shines through your creatures all speak to me of how awesome and beautiful you are, O God! Let my heart always be open to see and receive the good, and my hands be open to extend it to others. Teach me to live my life in you and for you.

Don't Be Afraid

If God is for us, who is against us? He who did not with-
hold his own Son, but gave him up for all of us, will he not
with him also give us everything else? . . . Who will separate
us from the love of Christ? Will hardship, or distress, or
persecution, or famine, or nakedness, or peril, or sword?
. . . No, in all these things we are more than conquerors
through him who loved us.

ROM 8:31–37

A follower of Christ must not be afraid. He feels wrapped in
an atmosphere of divine Providence that turns to good
even hostile things, which can also cooperate for our good, if we
love God (see Rom 8:28). He has a duty of witness, which frees
him from timidity and opportunism, and suggests to him, at
the right moment, an attitude and words, coming from an interior source, the existence of which was perhaps unknown to
him before the ordeal. Even if you are overcome by adversaries
stronger than yourselves, the Lord teaches us in the Gospel, "do
not worry about how you are to speak or what you are to say;
for what you are to say will be given to you at that time; for it is
not you who speak, but the Spirit of your Father speaking
through you." (Mt 10:19–20).

At this point there is a paradox to solve: are we not weak
owing to our infirm nature? Yes, it is true; even Jesus said so at

Gethsemane: "the flesh (that is, our human nature) is weak," but he affirmed at the same time that "the spirit indeed is willing" (Mt 26:41). Saint Paul explained that just when we humbly and realistically confess we are afflicted, then we are strong, because the Lord told him inwardly: "My grace is sufficient for you, for power is made perfect in weakness" (2 Cor 12:9–10). Weakness and strength, therefore, can be complementary in the Christian. . . .

The modern tendency to abolish all ethical or personal effort (except on the sports field, which is all very well, but is not enough) is not the prelude to real progress in the truly human sense. The Cross is always straight in front of us, and it summons us to moral strength, spiritual fortitude, and sacrifice (see Jn 12:25), which makes us like Christ and can save us and the world.

GENERAL AUDIENCE, MAY 28, 1975

I must admit, Lord, that sometimes I do feel afraid. I don't always remember that you are present within me, sustaining me in your love and strengthening me with your grace. How wonderful the truth of your ever-abiding presence and love is! Help me to live out of this certainty.

Believe in Christ

"Do not let your hearts be troubled. Believe in God, believe also in me. In my Father's house there are many dwelling places. If it were not so, would I have told you that I go to prepare a place for you? And if I go and prepare a place for you, I will come again and will take you to myself, so that where I am, there you may be also. And you know the way to the place where I am going." Thomas said to him, "Lord, we do not know where you are going. How can we know the way?" Jesus said to him, "I am the way, and the truth, and the life. No one comes to the Father except through me."

Jn 14:1–6

Our teacher is Christ.... "I am the way, and the truth, and the life" (Jn 14:6). Implicitly or explicitly, we place our faith in him for the simple fact that we bear his name: we are Christians. Christ indeed gave that wonderful, captivating description of himself. We can find it summarized in another description which Jesus also gave of himself, and which we could well keep in mind ...: "You have one Master, the Christ" (see Mt 23:10).

How many scriptural quotations we could recall to support and confirm this title of Master of life, which Jesus attributes not only to his mission but to his own Person. He is the Word, he is the Divine Word of God. Let us remember, for example, the mysterious voice that came from the bright cloud that appeared on the night of the Transfiguration: "This is my Son, the Beloved; with him I am well pleased; listen to him!" (Mt 17:5). Can we say that we are truly disciples of our Divine Master? Are we in conscience certain of being listeners who really give weight to his teaching? (see Mt 13:13–17). . . .

We must give or, if need be, restore to the name of "Christian" a genuine consistency with Christ's Word from which it is derived: this is the renewal we continue to seek. The condition and the consequence is this: listen to the Master, Christ.

Unfortunately, it is not hard to see that our standing as Christians, our Christian conscience, is often watered down by our way of living, which has made us forget its theological and ontological value, the concern for the state of faith—that state of grace, which is truly the Life of our life (cf. Rom 1:17; Gal 3:11). How many Christians are dominated by habits of thought and conduct copied from the world, to the detriment of the concept of our existence based upon the teaching of Jesus, our Master!

GENERAL AUDIENCE, AUGUST 20, 1975

Jesus Master, I believe in you. Make me a true disciple—not merely in words, but in how I live my life. The standards of the world are so different from those you preached. Grant me the courage to be true to who I am—a Christian, a follower of you, Lord. You are my Way, my Truth, and my Life.

Immersed in God

> When I look at your heavens, the work of your fingers,
>   the moon and the stars that you have established;
> what are human beings that you are mindful of them,
>   mortals that you care for them?
> Yet you have made them a little lower than God,
>   and crowned them with glory and honor. . . .
> O LORD, our Sovereign,
> how majestic is your name in all the earth!
>
>   Ps 8:3–5, 9

A fish cannot disregard the water in which it finds itself; nor can we disregard the atmosphere we breathe and in which our present existence takes place. God is the ineffable but real "element" in which our life has its origin, norm, and term: it is immersed in God. Let the listener exult: God is love, an ocean of love.

In other words, we must return to the thought of God, to the positive fact of religion, and we must give our religious faith the place and function due to it in a wise and organic conception of our life. Religion does not hinder our secular activity; it respects it, promotes it, rectifies it, and sanctifies it. It is, as it were, the lamp lit in the darkness of the room of our experience. The darkness disappears and the room acquires its shape, its colors, its beauty. Any deformities it has are, to the advantage of the person living in the room, revealed and can be repaired. God is light: "The Lord is my light and my salvation: whom shall I fear?" says the well-known Psalm 27. . . .

That means, therefore, that we must never blush, for fear of what people may say, at being people who believe in God and in Christ. We must not be people who need "all purpose" and all-expressive profane slogans to reveal and profess our superior system of thinking and acting. We ourselves, who believe in religion and seek in it the supreme reasons of our existence, must always be in an exploring and contemplative search of God and of Christ the revealer. We must nourish in ourselves a personal religious activity on the paths laid down by the Church, our teacher, and opening on to the infinite and beatifying mystery of God. To meditate, to pray—to pray means to ascend, to ascend to the first source of everything: of being, thought, action, enjoyment. [. . .] Let God's own Spirit help us to pray, to ascend!

GENERAL AUDIENCE, SEPTEMBER 17, 1975

God of my life, I am immersed in the ocean of your love—that love which surrounds me and nurtures me. You are the source of my being. Strengthen my faith; ground me in love so that I radiate you in all I do and say. Let me be your presence and your light in this world that so greatly needs you.

LOVE

"Love alone makes Christ the Savior and only through love can we approach him."

God Loves Us!

But now thus says the LORD,
 he who created you, O Jacob,
 he who formed you, O Israel:
Do not fear, for I have redeemed you;
 I have called you by name, you are mine.
When you pass through the waters, I will be with you;
 and through the rivers, they shall not overwhelm you;
when you walk through fire you shall not be burned,
 and the flame shall not consume you. . . .
Because you are precious in my sight,
and honored, and I love you.

ISA 43:1–4

Love God! A great word! A great law! But is it easy? Is it possible for us, children of our age? God. How can we know him? We are more accustomed to doubting him than thinking about him. . . .

How can the religious aridity of our times still admit that the most important and binding act of our life is love of God? . . . Love that is a quest, love that is expectation, love that is ascent, love that is joy, love that is light, love that is gift, love that is praise, love that is friendship, love that is bliss? . . .

Yes, God exists! But it is a tormenting certainty if it is not completed by the revelation that God made of himself. It is an extremely delicate and almost jealous revelation, because it is reserved for those who are ready to receive it with a limpid heart. Faith fills with light and joy the infinite space discovered by reason, and by the heart as God's country. It is then that Christ's intoxicating words reach us: "Our Father in heaven" (Mt 6:9).

Here then is the great conquest, the dimensions of which we can never explore enough: God is Father! This existential, metaphysical, unique, original, ineffable concept is the source of our religion, which lays down the following principle: if God is Father, God is Love. He loves us. We will never cease to satisfy every aspiration of our mind, our heart, and our spirit by letting this conviction penetrate us: we are loved! Loved by God! Everything is well for us if God loves us! And he does! Here, then, is the solution, at least the potential one, to our great problem: if God loves me, I cannot but love him. God's charity for us rebounds—as far as is granted to us by his grace—rebounds strongly, sincerely, humanly, happily, in our answer to him. Yes, O Lord, I, too, you know it, I, too, love you!

GENERAL AUDIENCE, NOVEMBER 11, 1975

God, my Father, how beautiful is the affirmation, "I love you," which you speak to me through the gift of your Word! Your love fills me with happiness and with purpose. It gives me courage in facing life's hardships. Help me never to forget your love, and let my love for you grow more and more.

God IS Love

Beloved, let us love one another, because love is from God;
everyone who loves is born of God and knows God.
Whoever does not love does not know God, for God is
love. God's love was revealed among us in this way: God
sent his only Son into the world so that we might live
through him. In this is love, not that we loved God but that
he loved us and sent his Son to be the atoning sacrifice for
our sins.

1 Jn 4:7–10

God is Love (see 1 Jn 4:8, 16; Jn 3:16). This is the
extreme revelation about God, which appears in the
darkness of denial and despair, in the clouds of ignorance
and doubt, in the flashes of fear and terror before God the
judge and vindicator, in all the amazement of a truth so
unexpected and dazzling: God is Love! This centrality of
God's love for us has expressions that go beyond every
dimension and all capacity of comprehension (see Eph
3:17–19). It offers us ineffable meetings with the Divinity,
still mysterious, but now accessible on a supernatural plane,
which raises the natural one to unhoped for fortunes, as in
the incarnation (Jn 3:16), in the redemption (2 Thes 2:16),
in the Eucharist (Jn 6:32), in Pentecost, and in the whole
economy of grace (Rom 8:30; 1 Jn 3:1).

We are loved by God! This is a revelation, a discovery that lies at the basis of the New Testament. From being a mere notion, it must become the structural hinge of our whole religious and moral outlook. We must make our own, deeply, the words of the Evangelist John, in his first Epistle: "So we have known and believe the love that God has for us" (4:16), *credimus caritati*; and therefore, a reciprocity, however disproportionate, is necessary: "We love, because he first loved us" (1 Jn 4:19).

Here the logic of love demands love from us! . . . Christ calls it a *new commandment*, because of a "just as" that extends its measure beyond all measure: "I give you a new commandment, that you love one another. *Just as* I have loved you, you also should love one another." (Jn 13:34). In this way he introduced an irrepressible and inexhaustible source of charity, no longer specifically religious, but human, into the hearts of his followers. These should be the most generous and ingenious professional exponents of charity toward their neighbor, to the extent of enjoying ecstatically the painful and joyful exercise of charity, which contemplates in a suffering brother or sister the representative of Jesus Christ himself. Bossuet* says this charity is almost a sacrament—"*mihi fecistis*" (Mt 25:40), you did it to me.

GENERAL AUDIENCE, SEPTEMBER 3, 1975

---

* Jacques Bénigne Bossuet was a seventeenth-century French bishop and spiritual writer.

Holy, triune God, you are Love—Love who created me, Love who redeemed me, Love who sanctifies me. Everything you are and do is love and generates love. Help me to live as a true child and disciple by imitating your love in my relations with others. Grant me a generous and loving heart.

Respond to Divine Love

Come, you that are blessed by my Father, inherit the kingdom prepared for you from the foundation of the world;
for I was hungry and you gave me food, I was thirsty and
you gave me something to drink, I was a stranger and you
welcomed me, I was naked and you gave me clothing, I was
sick and you took care of me, I was in prison and you visited me. . . . Truly I tell you, just as you did it to one of the
least of these who are members of my family, you did it to
me.

MT 25:34–36, 40

God revealed himself mainly in Love. The whole history
of salvation is Love. The whole Gospel. We could quote
so many expressions of Holy Scripture in this connection.
One comes to my lips from the Old Testament: "the LORD
appeared to him from far away. I have loved you with an everlasting love; therefore I have continued my faithfulness to
you" (Jer 31:3). The whole epic of the redemption is love,
compassion, the effusion of God's charity toward us. And the
story of Christ is summed up in Saint Paul's famous synthesis:
"I live by faith in the Son of God, who loved me and gave himself for me" (Gal 2:20). It is necessary to understand! I
recommend to attentive spirits another marvelous page of the
Apostle: "that you may have the power to comprehend, with
all the saints, what is the breadth and length and height and

depth, and to know the love of Christ that surpasses knowledge, so that you may be filled with all the fullness of God (Eph 3:18–19)....

And it therefore affects us, moves us, overwhelms us. If anyone succeeds in understanding that he or she has been loved, loved to a supreme and unthinkable degree, unto death—a silent, gratuitous, cruel death suffered until complete consummation (see Jn 19:30)—by one we did not even know, and when we knew him we denied and offended him; if anyone, I say, realizes they are the object of such a love, of so great a love, they can no longer remain tranquil. Dante, too, said so: "Love, that exempts no one beloved from loving" (*Inf.* 5, 103)....

Jesus loved us, the Council says, also with "a man's heart" (*Gaudium et Spes*, n. 22). And how he loved us! . . . Do you know this? Do you think of it? How do you intend to respond?

GENERAL AUDIENCE, JUNE, 2, 1969

Jesus, loving Master, your life is one great lesson in love! You say to me, "As I have done, so are you to do." I desire to follow you in the way of love by reaching out to those who need my help, listening to those who need understanding, resonating with those who need compassion, and encouraging those who need to be urged on. Help me always remember that it is you inviting me in my brother and sister.

Love Is the Art of Peace

"You have heard that it was said, 'An eye for an eye and a tooth for a tooth.' But I say to you, Do not resist an evildoer. But if anyone strikes you on the right cheek, turn the other also; and if anyone wants to sue you and take your coat, give your cloak as well; and if anyone forces you to go one mile, go also the second mile. Give to everyone who begs from you, and do not refuse anyone who wants to borrow from you."

Mt 5:38–42

Love that is charity brings about reconciliation. It is a creative act in the web of human relations. Love overcomes dissensions, jealousies, dislikes, age-old oppositions and those newly emerging. Love gives peace its true root, and banishes hypocrisy, uncertainty, and egoism. Love is the art of peace. It introduces a new kind of teaching, one that involves a totally revised approach if we consider how—from the games children play right up to certain tracts on ethnology and the philosophy of history—fighting, conflict, the balance of power, and the usefulness of violence all seem to constitute a necessity, a badge of honor, and a source of self-interest. Above all, will love, Christian love, succeed in tearing from the heart's depths the poisoned and tenacious root of revenge—the "settling of accounts," the "eye for an eye" and "a tooth for a tooth" (see Mt 5:38)—from which bloodshed, reprisals, and destruction follow and are linked in a chain reaction, like an unending obligation of ignoble honor? . . .

Yes, love will succeed, because Jesus Christ has taught us so. He included the obligation to love in the prayer par excellence, the "Our Father," obliging our stubborn lips to repeat the wonderful words of forgiveness: "And forgive us our trespasses as we forgive those who trespass against us." Reconciling love is not weakness, nor cowardice; it demands strong, noble, generous, and sometimes even heroic feelings. It calls for overcoming oneself rather than one's enemy. It may at times even seem like dishonor—think of turning "the other cheek" to the person who has already struck you on one cheek (see Lk 6:29); think of giving your cloak to one who takes you to court and would have your tunic (see Mt 5:40). But it will never be an outrage to due justice or a renunciation of the right of the poor. In reality, reconciling love will be the patient and wise art of peace, of wishing well to one another, of living together as brothers and sisters after the example of Christ and with the strength of our heart modeled on his.

HOMILY, WORLD DAY OF PEACE, JANUARY 1, 1975

Merciful Lord, with Saint Francis I pray, "Make me an instrument of your peace." Fill my heart with love that is patient, kind, and merciful—not arrogant, rude, resentful, or irritable—so that I may be an ambassador of your peace and reconciling love, here, where you have placed me.

EUCHARIST

"The Eucharistic Mystery is essentially the mystery of the Real Presence of Jesus and of the real memorial of his passion."

Mystery of Love

"I have eagerly desired to eat this Passover with you before I suffer; for I tell you, I will not eat it until it is fulfilled in the kingdom of God." Then he took a cup, and after giving thanks he said, "Take this and divide it among yourselves; for I tell you that from now on I will not drink of the fruit of the vine until the kingdom of God comes." Then he took a loaf of bread, and when he had given thanks, he broke it and gave it to them, saying, "This is my body, which is given for you. Do this in remembrance of me."

Lᴋ 22:15–19

The Lord is saying: "Remember, I am with you always" (Mt 28:20). I am here, he is saying, because this is my Body! This is the cup of my Blood!

The mystery of his presence is thus enacted and celebrated: the mystery of his sacramental, but real and living presence. Jesus, the Teacher of humanity, is here; he is calling for you (see Jn 11:28).

Yes, he is calling you, each one by name! The mystery of the Eucharist is, above all, a personal mystery: personal because of his divine presence—the presence of Christ, the Word of God made man—personal, because the Eucharist is meant for each of us. For this Christ has become living bread, and is multiplied in the sacrament, in order to be accessible to every human being who receives him worthily, and who opens to him the door of faith and love.

The Eucharist is a mystery of life! Christ says: "Whoever eats of this bread will live forever!" (Jn 6:51). The Eucharist is a mystery of suffering, yes; and a mystery of death; a mystery of redemptive passion; a mystery of sacrifice that has been consummated by Christ for our salvation. It is the mystery of the Cross, reflected and commemorated in the sacrament that makes us share in the Lord's immolation, to associate us in his resurrection. Today, in time, the Eucharist is the food for our earthly pilgrimage. Tomorrow, in the life to come, it will be our everlasting happiness.

The Eucharist is, therefore, a mystery of love. It makes all of us who eat the same bread into a single body (see 1 Cor 10:17), living by means of one Spirit. It makes us one family: brothers and sisters united in solidarity with one another (see Eph 4:16), and all of us dedicated to giving witness, in mutual love, to the fact that we really are the followers of Christ. May it always be this way!

MESSAGE TO FORTY-FIRST INTERNATIONAL
EUCHARISTIC CONGRESS, AUGUST 8, 1976

Jesus, how inventive your love is! You promised to remain with us and have done so through the mystery of the Eucharist. I adore you present in your Body and Blood, the source of my life. Grant me a great love for the Sacrifice of the Mass and for your presence in the Blessed Sacrament; let me receive you often in Holy Communion.

Extraordinary Bread

I am the bread of life. Your ancestors ate the manna in the wilderness, and they died. This is the bread that comes down from heaven, so that one may eat of it and not die. I am the living bread that came down from heaven. Whoever eats of this bread will live forever; and the bread that I will give for the life of the world is my flesh."

Jɴ 6:48–51

Man is a being that hungers and thirsts. He is a being that is not self-sufficient. . . . That is why he desires, studies, works, wills, suffers, prays, hopes, awaits. . . . We are living beings who need bread, a bread that will nourish and complete us, a bread that will broaden and lengthen our ever-craving and perishable existence. . . . There is no bread on earth to satisfy it: there is no bread from earth to make it immortal.

And here we have the divine word of the Lord Jesus: "I am the bread of life. . . . Whoever eats of this bread will live forever" (Jn 6:48, 50). . . .

Yes, let us remember this well: Christ is the bread of life. . . . Just as ordinary bread is meant for earthly hunger, so Christ is the extraordinary bread intended for the extraordinary and limitless hunger of men and women—able and most anxious indeed to open their hearts to infinite longings. We often have the temptation to think that Christ does not really fit in with our needs, desires, and destinies.... Many have succeeded in satisfying themselves with conquests other than those of faith, or imagine that religion is unreal nourishment, empty and useless in practice.

Christ does not cover himself with the appearances of food to deceive our higher hunger. Rather, he takes on the appearances of material food to have us desire him as the spiritual food that he is.... It is he who extended the incomparable invitation: "Come to me, all you that are weary and are carrying heavy burdens, and I will give you rest" (Mt 11:28). It is he who, no longer under the appearances of bread and wine, but under the appearances of every suffering and needy human being will reveal on the last day—the day of judgment—that every time we have helped someone, we have helped him—Christ: "For I was hungry and you gave me food, I was thirsty and you gave me something to drink" (Mt 25:35).

Thus, for us the Eucharist becomes not only food for our souls and our communities, but also the incentive of love for all our brothers and sisters who need help, understanding, and solidarity, thus enriching social action with energy, idealism, and hope that will never be extinguished, as long as Christ is with us in his Eucharist. Christ is the bread of life. Christ is necessary for every person, for every community, for every reality of a truly social nature—founded, that is, on love and on self-sacrifice—and for the world. Like bread, Christ is necessary!

Message to Forty-First International
Eucharistic Congress, August 8, 1976

Lord Jesus, it comes spontaneously for me to say, "Give us this bread always!" How close you have made yourself through this personal gift of your Body and Blood! Remain with me and strengthen me on my pilgrim way; transform my thoughts, words, and deeds into signs of your presence for everyone whose life I touch today.

Real Presence

I received from the Lord what I also handed on to you, that the Lord Jesus on the night when he was betrayed took a loaf of bread, and when he had given thanks, he broke it and said, "This is my body that is for you. Do this in remembrance of me." In the same way he took the cup also, after supper, saying, "This cup is the new covenant in my blood. Do this, as often as you drink it, in remembrance of me." For as often as you eat this bread and drink the cup, you proclaim the Lord's death until he comes.

1 Cor 11:23–26

In the sacrament of the Eucharist the Lord presents himself to us not as he is, but as he wishes us to consider him, as he wishes us to approach him. He offers himself to us under the aspect of expressive signs that he himself chose. It is as if he said: *Look at me in this way, get to know me like this. The signs of the bread and the wine tell you what I wish to be for you.* He speaks to us by means of these signs, and says: *This is how I am among you now.*

Therefore, though we cannot enjoy his tangible presence, we can and ought to enjoy his Real Presence under these significant forms. What is Jesus' intention in giving himself to us in the Eucharist? Oh! If we think about it well, we shall see that his intention is most patient! It tells us many, many things about Jesus. Above all, it tells us about his love. It tells us that although Jesus conceals himself in the Eucharist, he also reveals himself in it, reveals himself in love. The "mystery of faith" opens up as the "mystery of love." Think of it. This is the sacramental garb that at the same time hides and reveals Jesus, bread and wine, given for us. Jesus gives himself, presents himself. This is the center, the focal point of the whole of the Gospel, of the incarnation, of the redemption. *Born for us, given for us.*

For each of us? Yes, for each of us. Jesus has multiplied his real but sacramental presence in time and number, to be able to offer each of us—we mean each of us—the good fortune, the joy to approach him, and to be able to say: "He is for me, he is mine." Saint Paul says that Christ "loved me and gave himself for me!" (Gal 2:20).

We must exclaim with Saint Augustine: "O sacrament of goodness, O sign of unity, O bond of charity!" (In Jo. Tr. 26, PL 35, 1613). Infinite light, radiant love, flows out from the Real Presence. It is a radiation of permanent love, of universal love. Neither time nor space puts limits to it.

HOMILY, FEAST OF CORPUS CHRISTI, MAY 28, 1970

Jesus, Redeemer, present as food in the most holy Eucharist, fill my life with your presence. Earthly food is changed into the Body, but your gift of divine food changes us into yourself. The living Host plants a seed of resurrection and immortality in my being that increases my desire for you. It is both hope and promise. I praise you for this tremendous gift!

Mystery of Faith

Those who eat my flesh and drink my blood have eternal life, and I will raise them up on the last day; for my flesh is true food and my blood is true drink.... When many of his disciples heard it, they said, "This teaching is difficult; who can accept it?" ...

Jesus asked the twelve, "Do you also wish to go away?" Simon Peter answered him, "Lord, to whom can we go? You have the words of eternal life. We have come to believe and know that you are the Holy One of God."

JN 6:54–55, 60, 67–69

The Eucharist is a mystery of presence due to love. Jesus said, "I will not leave you orphaned. I am coming to you," letting it be understood that his temporal life was approaching its end. This is a delightful promise, which after the resurrection becomes solemn, and marks the destiny and reality of our religious and human history. "I am with you always, to the end of the age" (Mt 28:20). God with us; Christ with us! The whole of Christianity is a fact, a mystery, of Presence.... Where the Eucharist is celebrated, this "mystery of faith" is revealed and proclaimed: Jesus is here, Christ our Savior, alive and real. He is present! When we let this sweet and tremendous truth enter our consciousness we can no longer remain indifferent, impassive, and complacent. He is here!

Our first feeling is one of adoration and exultation . . . almost of confusion. What are we to do? What are we to say? Sing? Weep? Pray? Or perhaps we should be silent and contemplate like Mary, the sister of Martha? Martha was agitated and anxious to serve the Lord, while Mary "sat at the Lord's feet and listened to what he was saying" (Lk 10:39). Eucharistic adoration comes into being here.

But a second feeling creeps over us, the feeling of legitimate curiosity. Our faith assures us: Christ is present, alive, true, real. Then a series of questions arises in our mind. He is present? But how? Where? And why? Does he let himself be seen, approached, touched, as by the people in the Gospel (see 1 Jn 1:1)? He is hidden, but can he be identified? . . . How can he be food, on which people can nourish themselves? Are bread and wine changed into flesh and blood, just like Jesus, as he was on the Cross? "This teaching is difficult!" (Jn 6:60). Theology on the Eucharist arises from this point.

Yes, it is hard. But you know that Jesus was inflexible in demanding that his great speech on the Eucharistic mystery should be taken literally (see Jn 6:61ff). It is necessary to believe. To believe in the Word and on the word of Christ is a mystery of faith. . . . The fact is that . . . under the species of bread and wine, a Reality is hidden, which takes the place of the substance of the bread and wine. This Reality is Jesus himself, in a word, clothed in those humble appearances.

HOMILY, CORPUS CHRISTI, JUNE 13, 1974

Loving Lord, I believe that you are truly present—body, blood, soul, and divinity—in the most holy Eucharist. I adore you in your sacrament. You are the Living Bread come down from heaven. Nourish me with your Body and your word. Increase my faith and enflame my heart with burning love for you. Transform me into bread, broken and shared for others.

MARY,
OUR MOTHER

"Everything in Mary is an example for us."

Devotion to Mary

In the sixth month the angel Gabriel was sent by God to a town in Galilee called Nazareth, to a virgin engaged to a man whose name was Joseph, of the house of David. The virgin's name was Mary. And he came to her and said, "Greetings, favored one! The Lord is with you." But she was much perplexed by his words and pondered what sort of greeting this might be. The angel said to her, "Do not be afraid, Mary, for you have found favor with God. And now, you will conceive in your womb and bear a son, and you will name him Jesus."

LK 1:26–31

I feel we must seek to understand anew the reasons for our veneration and trust for Our Lady. Do we need this? Yes, we all need it. . . .

Devotion to Our Lady does not always find our minds so disposed, inclined, and contented with professing it in the depths of our hearts as it once did. . . .

How did Christ come among us? Did he come of himself? Did he come without any relationship with or any cooperation on the part of humanity? Can he be known, understood, and contemplated in abstraction from any real, historical, and existential relationships which his appearance in the world necessarily implies? Clearly not. The mystery of Christ is made part of a divine plan of human sharing. He came among us by following the way of human generation. He wished to have a Mother. He wished to take flesh through the vital cooperation of a woman, of her who is blessed among all women. The Apostle who outlined the fundamental theological structure of Christianity said: "When the fullness of time had come, God sent his Son, born of a woman . . ." (Gal 4:4). And the Council reminds us that Mary was "used by God not merely in a passive way," but "cooperated in the work of human salvation through free faith and obedience" (*Lumen Gentium*, 56). It is then no negligible, secondary chance circumstance, but an essential part, one that is of the greatest importance, beauty, and comfort for us human beings, that Christ came to us through Mary. We received him from her. We encounter him as the flower of humanity, opening on the immaculate and virginal stem that is Mary, "thus it was that this flower budded forth" (Dante, *Par.* 33, 9). If we wish to be followers of Christ, we must be followers of Mary, that is to say, we must recognize the essential life-giving and providential relationship linking Our Lady with Jesus, and opening up to us the way that leads to him. It is a twofold way: the way of example and the way of intercession.

HOMILY, APRIL 24, 1970

Mary, you are the mother of Jesus and my mother. Draw me to your maternal heart and teach me to follow Christ as you followed him. Strengthen in me the desire to love and serve him always, to always say yes to all that he asks. Obtain for me an intimate relationship with your Divine Son.

Look to Mary

"My soul magnifies the Lord,
    and my spirit rejoices in God my Savior,
for he has looked with favor on the lowliness of his servant.
    Surely, from now on all generations will call me
        blessed;
for the Mighty One has done great things for me,
and holy is his name."

                                                Lᴋ 1:46–49

D o we want to be Christians, that is, imitators of Christ? Let us look to Mary. She is the most perfect example of likeness to Christ. She is the "type." She is the image that reflects Christ better than any other. She is the "excellent exemplar in faith and in charity" (*Lumen Gentium,* 53, 61, 65, etc.). How sweet, how consoling it is for us who wish to walk in the footsteps of the Lord to have before us Mary, her image, her remembrance, her kindness, her humility and purity, her greatness. How close to us the Gospel is in the power that Mary personifies and radiates with human and superhuman splendor! When we draw close to her any fear we would have is dissipated—fear that in marking our spirituality with devotion to Mary, our religious sense, our vision of life, and our moral energy would become soft, weak, and almost infantile. She is the poetess and prophetess of redemption, and we hear from her pure lips the strongest and most original hymn ever uttered—the "Magnificat"! She reveals the transforming design of the Christian economy, the historical and social result that still draws its origin and strength from Christianity. God, she sings, "has scattered the proud in the thoughts of their hearts. He has brought down the powerful from their thrones, and lifted up the lowly" (Lk 1:51–52).

At this point a second way is opened for us by Our Lady, so that we may reach our salvation in the Lord Christ: it is her protection. She is our ally, our advocate. She is the confidence of the poor, of the lowly, of the suffering. She is even the "refuge of sinners." She has a mission of pity, goodness, and intercession for all. She consoles every grief of ours. She teaches us to be good, to be strong, and to be compassionate toward all. She is the queen of peace. She is the Mother of the Church.

HOMILY, APRIL 24, 1970

Mary, your life is an inspiration to me. Your kindness, humility, purity, your obedience to the will of the Lord are all examples for me. Help me to live my life in your company, with faith and trust in the saving power of God. Form me as you formed your Son, Jesus. My refuge in difficulties, my hope and comfort in this valley of tears, guide me through the pilgrimage of life.

Mother of Christ

Standing near the cross of Jesus were his mother, and his mother's sister, Mary the wife of Clopas, and Mary Magdalene. When Jesus saw his mother and the disciple whom he loved standing beside her, he said to his mother, "Woman, here is your son." Then he said to the disciple, "Here is your mother." And from that hour the disciple took her into his own home.

JN 19:25–27

Our Lady belongs wholly to Christ—in him, through him, with him. We cannot, even for an instant, forget this relationship that defines Mary, Mother of Jesus, animated and living by his Word, and the companion of his passion. This relationship gives reason for her every prerogative, for her every grandeur, for her every title to our unbounded veneration, to our love, to our trust. . . . No human creature has come nearer to Christ, none has been more his and more filled with grace than she. No one has been so closely united to Christ as his Mother. And no one has been so loved by Christ as she who gave him virginal birth by the power of the Holy Spirit, she who heard his Word with a "*fiat*" that marked Our Lady's whole life, she who was the willing participant in every mystery of Christ's salvific mission (see *Lumen Gentium*, n. 61). No one has had so great a faith in Christ (You remember?—"Blessed is she who believed,"—Lk 1:45). No one has had so great a trust as she in the beneficent goodness of Christ (see Jn 2:5). It is easy to believe that no one had so great a love for Christ as his Mother had, not only because of the ever incomparable love relation that a mother has with the fruit of her womb, but also because of the charity of the Holy Spirit. In her that charity was a vivifying and loving principle of her divine maternity, which associated her with the passion of her Son. At Pentecost her maternity overflowed in her heart and so dilated it as to make her the spiritual mother of the new-born Church. . . . Yes, blessed are you, Mary, to whom we now have the unmerited good fortune to give a title which the Christian centuries always recognized as yours, not in the sacramental order as a cause of grace, but in that of the widespread communion of charity and grace, proper to the Mystical Body—namely, the title "Mother of the Church." Thus does our devotion to Mary most holy spread out from its center in Christ throughout the Church.

GENERAL AUDIENCE, MAY 29, 1968

My loving Mother, like Jesus, I place myself entirely into your hands. Obtain for me the grace to know, love and more closely imitate him—my Way, my Truth, and my Life. Help me draw always nearer to him. Enlighten my mind, fortify my will, sanctify my heart, so that one day I may be able to say, "It is no longer I who live, but it is Christ who lives in me" (Gal 2:20).

The Rosary

When the day of Pentecost had come, they were all together in one place. And suddenly from heaven there came a sound like the rush of a violent wind, and it filled the entire house where they were sitting. Divided tongues, as of fire, appeared among them, and a tongue rested on each of them. All of them were filled with the Holy Spirit.

ACTS 2:1–4

I should like to talk about the Rosary. . . . A tormented, famous, spiritual, and realistic writer, Charles Péguy, compared the Our Father and the Hail Mary in the Rosary to ships sailing victoriously toward the Father (see *Le Mystère des Saints Innocents*, 1912). We too should attempt that mystic voyage. . . .

The prayer of petition in the ordinary intention of the person reciting the Rosary fuses and, as it were, transfuses into contemplative prayer through the attention the mind gives to the mysteries of the Rosary. These turn this pious Marian devotion into a meditation on Christ, and accustom us to look at him from the best possible viewpoint, that of Mary herself. The Rosary sets our gaze and our mind upon Christ, the scenes of his life and their theological meaning. It does this not only with Mary, but also in the same way as Mary, insofar as this is possible for us. There is no doubt that no one ever gave more thought to him (see Lk 2:19.51; 8:21; 11:28), understood him more, loved him more, and lived more like him.

Secondly, the Rosary puts anyone who has trust in it into communication with Our Lady, sets up a dialogue with her, and puts him beside her. It obliges one to feel her power, her evangelical style, and her example, which instructs and transforms. It is a school that makes us Christians. This benefit is almost an unexpected one, but how precious it is, and how close to our primary needs.

So listen, dearly beloved children, to my call to prayer. As we move along its line of repeated but meditative invocations, it strengthens us in hope; assimilates us to Christ; and obtains for us patience, peace, and the joy of Christ.

GENERAL AUDIENCE, SEPTEMBER 8, 1969

Dearest Lady of the Rosary, through the mysteries of the life, death, resurrection, and glory of your Divine Son, Jesus Christ, lead me into ever deeper relationship with the Divine Trinity, holiness of life, generosity in ministering to others. Teach me contemplation and be my protection against the assaults of the evil one.

Prayer

"The 'Our Father' is the simplest, happiest, and deepest expression of our religion."

Inner Silence

O LORD, my heart is not lifted up,
      my eyes are not raised too high;
I do not occupy myself with things
      too great and too marvelous for me.
But I have calmed and quieted my soul,
      like a weaned child with its mother;
my soul is like the weaned child that is with me.

Ps 131:1–2

What is our great problem? It is our relationship with God. Everything is here, in this tangle of mental, moral, spiritual, and vital questions. Our conception of life cannot disregard consideration of this relationship, whether we deny it, discuss it, or affirm it. These are the supreme and summary categories into which this problematic relationship can be placed. And everyone knows today that no one can avoid the necessity of a choice in this connection. In one way or another, religion is at the apex of our definition of our personal and collective life. Let us limit ourselves now to personal life. The most important qualifying distinctive note is drawn from the religious attitude that one professes concerning the conception of his or her own life. . . .

To grasp something of the religious problem, we need silence, inner silence, which also perhaps calls for a little external silence. By silence, we mean a pause amidst all the noise, all the impressions of the senses, all the voices, which the environment compels us to listen to, making us turn outward and deafening us. Meanwhile it fills us with echoes, images, and stimuli, which, whether we like it or not, paralyze our inner freedom to think and to pray. Silence here does not mean sleep. In our case it means a talk with ourselves, quiet reflection, an act of conscience, a moment of personal solitude, an attempt to recuperate ourselves.

We will go further and say: we will give silence the capacity of listening. Listening to what? To whom? We cannot say. But we know that spiritual listening allows us, if God grants us the grace, to hear his voice, that voice of his which is immediately distinguished by the sweetness and strength of the word of God. It is God whom we then, as if by instinctive impulse, begin to call within ourselves, with eagerness to know and understand, with anguish and with confidence, with unusual emotion, and with invading goodness; the God-Word, who has become our interior master.

General Audience, December 4, 1973

Divine Master, my ever-patient Teacher, teach me the way of loving and attentive silence. Let me be more aware of your indwelling, triune Presence in my soul. Silence the many voices that seek to distract me and lead me away from you; be the guiding voice in my life. May your Word draw me into a deeper and more intimate relationship with you, my God.

Need of Prayer

Jesus was praying in a certain place, and after he had finished, one of his disciples said to him, "Lord, teach us to pray, as John taught his disciples." He said to them, "When you pray, say:

Father, hallowed be your name.
Your kingdom come.
Give us each day our daily bread.
And forgive us our sins,
for we ourselves forgive everyone indebted to us.
And do not bring us to the time of trial."

Lk 11:1–4

How can we persuade the person of today to pray? And even before one prays, to have that perhaps vague, but deep, mysterious, and stimulating sense of God, which is the basis of prayer?

Prayer is conversation—a conversation carried on by our person with the invisible companion, of whose presence we have become aware. He is the holy Living One, who fills us with awe and love, the indescribable Godhead, whom Christ taught us to call Father through his priceless gift of revelation. By Father we mean the necessary and loving source of our life, he who is invisible and immense as the heavens, as the universe where he is, creating all, pervading all, continually working in all. . . .

We are aware of the enormous and increasing difficulty that people meet with (or *seem* to meet with) today in conversing with God. Call this phenomenon what you like: demythization, secularization, rationalism, self-sufficiency, . . . materialism. Whatever name it may have, it is still extremely grave, even though it may be quite simple in practice as it invades the masses, finds support and is propagated in culture and social life, getting in everywhere, as if it were an advance in thought and progress. . . .

Perhaps you remember Joergensen's "cord from above," a string holding up the whole web of life. If that cord is broken, all life sickens and declines, loses its true meaning, and its stupendous value. The cord is our relationship with God; it is religion. It holds us up and makes us experience a very rich range of sentiments: the marvel of existing, the joy and the responsibility of living. I am quite certain of this. . . .

Children of this century, I understand your difficulties, especially those in the psychological order, and this increases my interest and my love for you. I want to help you, to offer you that "supplement of spirit" that is lacking from the gigantic structure of modern life. . . .

The important thing is to find the way back to life, and that can only be found in contact with God. Do think about it again.

General Audience, August 27, 1969

Lord Jesus, with the disciples I beg you, teach me to pray. Teach me to pray with the confidence of a child, the docility of a disciple, and the ardor and abandonment of a lover. Let my prayer be both intimate conversation and profound contemplation, the savoring of your divine presence in my life. May my own prayer, O Lord, inspire others to turn to you in prayer as well.

Jesus Prays

Now during those days Jesus went out to the mountain to
pray; and he spent the night in prayer to God. And when
day came, he called his disciples and chose twelve of them,
whom he also named apostles.

Lᴋ 6:12–13

How and when did Jesus pray? O, how beautiful and
instructive an excursion into the Gospel pages would
be, picking like wild flowers the almost incidental references
to the Lord's prayer! The evangelist Mark writes: "In the
morning, while it was still very dark, he [Jesus] got up and
went out to a deserted place, and there he prayed" (1:35). See,
for example, after the multiplication of the loaves: "And after
he had dismissed the crowds, he went up the mountain by
himself to pray. When evening came, he was there alone," (Mt
14:23).

The Lord's prayers, about which the Gospel informs us,
would deserve such long meditation. The famous one, for
example, in chapter eleven of Matthew, lets us enter the deepest secret of his life: "At that time Jesus said, 'I thank you,
Father, Lord of heaven and earth, because you have hidden
these things from the wise and the intelligent and have
revealed them to infants . . .'" (v.25). And what can we say of
the prayer that concludes the talk of the Last Supper? "Jesus

looked up to heaven and said, 'Father, the hour has come; glorify your Son so that the Son may glorify you' " (Jn 17:1–2).
We recall it: it is the prayer for unity: "that they may all be
one" (Jn 17:21–22). And then the triple groaning, heroic
prayer at Gethsemane, just before the passion: "Father, if you
are willing, remove this cup from me; yet, not my will but
yours be done" (Lk 22:42).

What a revelation not only of the drama of the Savior's
life, but also of the complexity and depth of human destinies,
which even in their most tragic and mysterious expressions
can be linked, by means of prayer, to the goodness, the mercy,
and the salvation deriving from God!

Pray, then, like Jesus. Pray intensely. Pray today, always in
the confident communion that prayer has established between
us and the Father. Because it is to a father, it is to *the* Father
that our humble voice is addressed.

GENERAL AUDIENCE, JUNE 16, 1976

*Jesus, before every decision, trial, and suffering, and in the face of
death, you prayed. You prayed for others and for yourself. Prayer
kept you constantly in communion with the Father and the Spirit; it was your source of strength and peace. Instill in me this same
spirit of prayer; let it become as natural to me as breathing, so
that I may always be united to you.*

Personal Prayer

[Jesus] entered a certain village, where a woman named Martha welcomed him into her home. She had a sister named Mary, who sat at the Lord's feet and listened to what he was saying. But Martha was distracted by her many tasks; so she came to him and asked, "Lord, do you not care that my sister has left me to do all the work by myself? Tell her then to help me." But the Lord answered her, "Martha, Martha, you are worried and distracted by many things; there is need of only one thing. Mary has chosen the better part, which will not be taken away from her."

Lᴋ 10:38–42

We note with regret that personal prayer is diminishing. This is threatening the liturgy itself with inner impoverishment, with exterior ritualism and purely formal practice of religion. Religious feeling can wither through lack of two characteristics that are indispensable for prayer: interiority and individuality. Everyone needs to learn to pray inside himself and by himself. The Christian needs to have personal prayer. Every soul is a temple. "Do you not know," says Saint Paul, "that you are God's temple and that God's Spirit dwells in you?" (1 Cor 3:16)

When do we enter this temple of our consciences to adore God present there? Shall we be empty souls, even though Christian souls? Souls who are not present to themselves and have forgotten that mysterious and indescribable appointment which God, the one and triune God, deigns to make with us, for filial and overflowing conversation inside our very selves? Do we not remember the last words of Our Lord at the Last Supper: "Those who love me will keep my word, and my Father will love them, and we will come to them and make our home with them" (Jn 14:23)? This is charity praying (Saint Augustine): Are our hearts inspired with charity, enabling us to conduct this inward personal prayer?

The *Ecclesia orans* [praying Church] is a choir of single, vivid, conscious, and loving voices. It is an interior spiritual undertaking, personal devotion, meditation worked out in one's own heart, a certain degree of thinking and worshipping, sighing and rejoicing contemplation. It is the Church's petition, and the Church is renewing itself and wishes us to be witnesses and apostles.

Let us listen to this hymn to Christ, to God. . . . Let us try to add our own humble voices, here and now, everywhere and at all times.

HOMILY, APRIL 22, 1970

Holy Spirit, Spirit of the Father and of the Son, you are present and living in me. You pray within me when I myself am at a loss for words (see Rom 8:26f) and your prayer is heard by the Father. Come, Divine Spirit, infuse in me an ever greater yearning and love for God that becomes prayer of adoration, praise, surrender, and atonement. Strengthen this bond of love in me.

JOY

"The believer, he who has succeeded in meeting the risen Christ, should always have within him the charism of joy."

God Is Our Happiness

O give thanks to the LORD, call on his name,
    make known his deeds among the peoples.
Sing to him, sing praises to him;
    tell of all his wonderful works.
Glory in his holy name;
    let the hearts of those who seek the LORD rejoice.
Seek the LORD and his strength;
seek his presence continually.

Ps 105:1–4

This, beloved sons and daughters, is the true, the great, the blessed message of our religion: God is our happiness. God is joy, God is beatitude, God is the fullness of life, not only in himself, but for us. God has revealed himself in love. He has made himself proportionate to our extreme aspirations. God has had a heart for every deficiency, for our every wickedness, for our every sin. God has offered himself to us as mercy, grace, salvation, as a joyful, glorious surprise (see Rom 9:23; Col 1:27; Titus 2:11). We must repeat the angel's announcement of Christmas: "Do not be afraid; for see—I am bringing you good news of great joy for all the people" (Lk 2:10). Yes, our religion, is a religion of salvation, a religion of joy. Do we not hear within us, like bells pealing gaily, the echo of the Apostle's exhortations to the Philippians: "Rejoice in the Lord always; again I will say, Rejoice" (4:4)?

This is the true religion, our religion, our spirituality—the joy of God. This is the gift that Christ brings us on being born into the world—the joy of God.

Now, here is today's question: shall we succeed in making the people of our time understand this religious message— God is joy, our joy? Who listens to us? Who really believes us? (see Rom 10:15–16). Perhaps we will not succeed. Men of thought, immersed in the problems of doubt, do not believe us; men of action, fascinated by the effort to conquer the earth, do not believe us; nor does the man in the street, intolerant of inner meditations. . . . This is the fate of the Gospel in humanity (the Gospel means precisely this: happy proclamation). God will remain a problem, he will remain negation for many people even though it [his message] rings out near them; indifference, apathy, deafness, hostility will extinguish the beatifying voice. . . . In reply to this we will repeat: God is joy!

GENERAL AUDIENCE, DECEMBER 20, 1972

Apart from you, O God, there is no happiness. In the womb of your mercy and love we were created to be an extension of that same love in this world. Living that, we experience and spread happiness around us; we will attain then eternal, unlimited happiness with you in heaven. I ask for the grace to seek my happiness in you alone, O Lord, and to radiate it now and forever.

Serene in Christ

"Very truly, I tell you, you will weep and mourn, but the world will rejoice; you will have pain, but your pain will turn into joy. When a woman is in labor, she has pain, because her hour has come. But when her child is born, she no longer remembers the anguish because of the joy of having brought a human being into the world. So you have pain now; but I will see you again, and your hearts will rejoice, and no one will take your joy from you."

JN 16:20–22

The Christian life is not without joy. In it we will find other elements besides joy—it includes the cross, renunciation, mortification, penitence, pain, sacrifice. But it never lacks a deep consolation, a sense of joy, which should never be lost, and is never lost when our souls are in God's grace. When God is with us can we be altogether sad, bitter, or desperate? No, the joy of God must always be, at least basically, a prerogative of the Christian soul. . . .

We Christians should not feel unhappier than other people because we have accepted Christ's yoke—a yoke that he bears with us and which he describes as "light and easy." On the contrary, we should feel happier than others, because we have splendid and secure reasons to be happier. Christ won salvation for us, and, through it, [we find] light on the most difficult problems of our existence. This justifies us in looking at everything with optimism.

We are better placed than others who lack the light of the Gospels, to view with happy wonder the panorama of life and the world. We can enjoy with grateful serenity whatever life has in store for us, even its frequent trials. The Christian is fortunate. He knows how to find proofs of the goodness of God in every event, in every aspect of history and experience. He knows that "all things work together for good for those who love God" (Rom 8:28). The Christian must always show forth his greater security, so that others may see from where he derives his serene spiritual superiority—the joy of Christ. . . . Christ is our happiness. Let us repeat this in his honor and for our comfort: Alleluia!

GENERAL AUDIENCE, APRIL 17, 1968

Jesus, you are my joy even in the midst of darkness and grief. The assurance of your love for me is my comfort. Your Cross is my strength. You give me direction in times of uncertainty and a sense of reassurance even in apparent failure. You are my happiness. I believe in you and place all my trust in you.

Easter Joy

The angel said to the women, "Do not be afraid; I know
that you are looking for Jesus who was crucified. He is not
here; for he has been raised, as he said. Come, see the place
where he lay. Then go quickly and tell his disciples, 'He has
been raised from the dead, and indeed he is going ahead of
you to Galilee; there you will see him.' This is my message
for you." So they left the tomb quickly with fear and great
joy, and ran to tell his disciples.

Mt 28:5–8

I am happy to announce Easter joy to you! The customary
wish of "Happy Easter!" is not an empty or conventional
greeting. Joy is a truly Christian heritage. This is true, with so
much reason and fullness as to constitute our ultimate, highest message. Happiness is our good news. Today this good
news, sung by the angels on Christmas night at the coming of
Christ to the world, and preached by Christ in his sermon on
the mount . . . resounds as a silver trumpet among God's people. It is the good news of the unheard of victory over sorrow,
sin, and death, won by Christ for himself, "the first fruits of
those who have died" (1 Cor 15:20) . . . and won by him for
us. . . .

Ours is a true and joyful message . . . by the invincible reasons on which it is founded: by reason of the infinite happiness
of God irradiating in love over the human panorama,

spreading over it those sparks that are signs and reminders of a higher fullness, and knocking at the door of man's heart through an inexpressible supernatural communion. [Ours is a true and joyful message . . .] by reason of the entire economy of salvation, offered to us precisely to free us from our more serious, and of themselves incurable interior miseries, our faults, and communicated to us to turn to good even the most negative things—pain poverty, weariness, disappointment, death. . . . These are true reasons and we must witness to them today. I repeat to you with the Apostle: "Rejoice in the Lord always; again I will say, Rejoice" (Phil 4:4). Be happy today for the celebration of this indescribable occurrence that concerns all of us and involves all of us, namely the resurrection of Christ.

Be happy, be joyful at this faith, at this good fortune, at this Easter hymn to life, to life that dies not and rises again, to life which, even in the temporal sphere, is illumined with new hope, able to make it dare the most arduous tasks and solve the most intricate problems.

General Audience, April 6, 1969

Your resurrection, Lord, fills me with joy, gratitude, and a sense of profound adoration. You have won victory over sin and death, and won for us the possibility of everlasting happiness in the beatific vision of heaven. With Thomas I exclaim, "My Lord and my God!" You are the joy of my life and my hope of salvation is in you.

Joy in the Church

Praise the LORD, all you nations!
    Extol him, all you peoples!
For great is his steadfast love toward us,
    and the faithfulness of the LORD endures forever.
    Praise the Lord!

                                        Ps 117

Alleluia means praise the Lord! And, like a song, it
expresses the joy and enthusiasm that sustains and
accompanies our pilgrimage, now safe, toward the fullness of
eternal life (see Saint Augustine, Sermon 255; PL 38,
1186)....

Rare are the moments in which one can be happy without
limits, without fears, without remorse. Remember the verses
of the psalm: "I was glad when they said to me, 'Let us go to
the house of the LORD!'" (Ps 122:1) And again: "How lovely
is your dwelling place, O LORD of hosts! My soul longs,
indeed it faints for the courts of the LORD" (Ps 84:1–2).
Religion, faith, grace have these moments of inner exultation,
these surprises of the Spirit, these sweet, impetuous preludes
of God's life in us. Yes, Alleluia, in Christ and in the Church.
"Joy, joy, tears of joy" (Pascal).

And if I repeat this cry of exuberant gladness, it is also
with a pastoral intention. The joy of a moment of plenitude,

both sensible and spiritual, is not sufficient. Joy must be perennial, even if it has a lower degree of intensity. The believer, who has succeeded in meeting the risen Christ, even though in the incognito of our earthly pilgrimage (see Lk 24:32), should always have within him the charism of joy. Joy, with peace, is the first fruit of the Spirit (Gal 5:22). And we know that in the divine plan of salvation there is a relationship between the Spirit and the Church. . . . To enjoy the joyful charism of the Spirit, it is necessary to love the Church. . . .

We hope, brothers and sisters, that, thinking of the Church, her history, her glories, her weaknesses, her needs, her real post-conciliar rebirth, you will always have on your lips and in your hearts the paschal cry: Alleluia!

GENERAL AUDIENCE, APRIL 25, 1970

Holy Spirit of God, you are the one who instills in us the joy of God. We know joy when we remain united to the Lord and embrace the Divine Will. Come, Holy Spirit, infuse in me docility to the will of God. Keep me in that will, reminding me of the promise of Jesus. Increase in me your peace and your joy.

COURAGE

"You may lack all things, but not Jesus on the Cross. He is with you."

Christianity Is Demanding

"Enter through the narrow gate; for the gate is wide and the road is easy that leads to destruction, and there are many who take it. For the gate is narrow and the road is hard that leads to life, and there are few who find it."

Mt 7:13–14

A comfortable, lax, subjective, purely liberating interpretation of the Gospel is in fashion; the Gospel which, when all is said and done, we rightly consider the fundamental code of our religion. Did not the Lord say: "My yoke is easy, and my burden is light"? (Mt 11:30). Did he not say of himself: "I am the good Shepherd"? (Jn 10:11) who, having a hundred sheep goes after that which is lost, until he finds it. . . . Yes, goodness, love, self-sacrifice, forgiveness are the essential characteristics of the Gospel. They faithfully delineate the profile of Christ. But we cannot forget another characteristic of his preaching: the kingdom of heaven, which Jesus Christ preached, is neither politically subversive, nor morally permissive (in the modern sense of the word). Jesus Christ is the great Prophet of human reform, the reform that is demanded by everyone and is salvation for everyone. . . .

We should reread the famous and fundamental Sermon on the Mount in the Gospel of Matthew. How often Jesus constructs his address with the dialectics of a reforming antithesis: "You have heard that it was said to those of ancient times . . ." (Mt 5:17.21ff), he affirms repeatedly; and then at once: "but I say to you. . . ." The kingdom of heaven, we can say Christianity, is demanding. It is a narrow gate that leads to life; it calls for an effort, it calls for commitment. It is not for the weak, the cowardly, or the pleasure-seekers. It is for the courageous, the strong, for those who do not refuse to carry the Cross with Christ, like Christ.

What this Cross is, the Gospel again will tell us: it will be the sense of moral duty, of spiritual interiority, of brotherly, social love. It will be that persistent effort of self-reform, by means of which we give our life a content and an aspect of Christian authenticity, let us even say of holiness, knowing that divine grace helps us to reach this great goal.

GENERAL AUDIENCE, SEPTEMBER 8, 1975

To be a Christian, Lord Jesus, is to live as you lived—that's a big order for anyone! But you promised that all things are possible with your grace. With this confidence I ask you for the grace to be faithful in following you and carrying out the will of the Father, even when it means embracing the Cross.

Live by Hope

We are always confident; even though we know that while we are at home in the body we are away from the Lord—for we walk by faith, not by sight. Yes, we do have confidence, and we would rather be away from the body and at home with the Lord. So whether we are at home or away, we make it our aim to please him. For all of us must appear before the judgment seat of Christ, so that each may receive recompense for what has been done in the body, whether good or evil.

2 Cor 5:6–10

If hope does not sustain us, our perseverance is not certain. We might lose our way, and it is so easy to do so today, unfortunately. It is easy to renounce the ideals of Christian life. . . . Opportunism is fashionable. . . . Near and personal success takes the place of the ideal. . . . The enthusiasm of resistance, courage, and sacrifice is replaced by calculation of usefulness; acceptance of fashion; confidence in the majority; unwillingness to play the part of having a precise, strong, and difficult personality of one's own. . . . There is no longer a place for hope that goes beyond the present-day limits of the experimental world. "*(Seize the day)*," do not miss the passing moment and the reality that can be enjoyed today, is the great principle, the one commandment, the truth of our existence because, according to this common and atrocious concept of life, there is nothing else! It is materialism, which degrades life to the animal level without transcendent hopes. It is agnosticism, satisfied with shortsightedness and its insoluble doubts. . . .

In the realistic view of faith which is the basis of hope (see Heb 11:1), a whole universe surrounds the believer, a pilgrim on earth and in time. The light, the providence, the goodness of God unfolds inestimable treasures. A part of these are already granted and enjoyed now. And a part, the larger part, are promised to those who make themselves worthy of them by grace that is always divine, and are able to wait for them, desire them, and hope for them. Without destroying present human hopes, the infallible and incomparable hopes of the Christian cosmos are superimposed on the brief, uncertain, and deceptive hopes of those who think of constructing a pagan and materialistic humanism. [In the Christian cosmos] death itself, the last terrible enemy, thought to be invincible (see 1 Cor 15:26), surrenders to Christ's glorious life, which we have been solemnly promised (see *Lumen Gentium,* 48).

The world needs this hope, which is set above human suffering, above hunger and thirst for justice, which is inscribed over our tombs. We must live by it.

GENERAL AUDIENCE, DECEMBER 10, 1975

My hope, O Lord, is in you. You are my Way, my Truth, my Life; my one and supreme good. Help me to never lose sight of my ultimate destination or be detoured by the maze of slogans clamoring for my attention. Keep my heart and my gaze fixed on you, who give meaning to everything in and around me.

The Christian Lifestyle

"If any want to become my followers, let them deny themselves and take up their cross daily and follow me. For those who want to save their life will lose it, and those who lose their life for my sake will save it. What does it profit them if they gain the whole world, but lose or forfeit themselves?"

Lk 9:23–25

There are those who think they can content themselves with Christ, but without the obligation of contemplating his Cross, or of admitting his resurrection, and moreover without entering the sacramental and moral experience of our participation in this paschal and central mystery of death and life, which is supernatural.

And there are those who think they can make up for the immense void left by this residual spirituality without real and existential redemption, by adopting another "*without.*" That is, [that they somehow have the ability to remove] from their own lives every barrier, every distinction from the life of the profane world, [and that they can do so] without hope, without charity, without morals that are firm and worthy.

Instead, they trust in the ideologies of others (while drawing to a certain extent on that treasure of human wisdom, the Gospel) to make the person himself, his own personality, and society itself, the ideal—nay more the idol to which the mental and civil processes of life are directed. But without God what life can endure?

Beloved sons and daughters! Let us maintain the desire for a life modeled after the Christian lifestyle. The Christian lifestyle is not always easy. It is, we know, a demanding style of living, sometimes inconvenient, and not always fashionable. But remember: it must not be judged only by what it takes away, but evaluated by what it gives. And if it is engraved on us by the law of sacrifice, that is, by the Cross, remember, or rather, experience for yourselves the paradox characteristic of the Christian way of life. It consists in an extraordinary and simultaneous fusion of braking and thrusting, of moderation and vitality, of sorrow and joy. The present life finds in this lifestyle its highest and fullest expression, as Saint Paul said: "I am overjoyed in all our affliction" (2 Cor 7:4).

May God help all of us impress on our modern life a new style, sweet and austere, the Christian lifestyle.

GENERAL AUDIENCE, NOVEMBER 22, 1972

Jesus Master, living the Gospel is not always easy and I often find myself challenged in living humility, patience, gentleness, and reconciliation, and bearing with one another in love. But with you, all things are possible and you have promised every grace to those who ask. So I ask you to help me live, generously and unafraid, the Christian life as you modeled it.

Christ Is for Us

"Come to me, all you that are weary and are carrying heavy
burdens, and I will give you rest. Take my yoke upon you,
and learn from me; for I am gentle and humble in heart,
and you will find rest for your souls. For my yoke is easy,
and my burden is light.

Mt 11:28–30

Why does the crucified Jesus attract us? O! How deeply
this question delves into our hearts!

It appears to me that the first reason is the solidarity, the
kinship, the sympathy which he, suffering and dying on the
Cross, has established with every person who suffers. Looking
at him, one seems to hear again this most human invitation:
"Come, come to me, all you that are weary and are carrying
heavy burdens, and I will give you rest" (Mt 11:28). Do we
ourselves listen to this voice, which comes from the dying lips
of Christ? In different ways and in various degrees, we are all
sufferers. Perhaps we don't hear this invitation to come to him
from "the man of suffering and acquainted with infirmity"
(Isa 53:3). In the natural world suffering is an isolated thing,
but for Jesus it is a point of encounter, of communion. Will
you think on it, brothers and sisters? You who are sick, who
are unfortunate? You who are dying? Will you think on it, you
who are weighed down by fatigue, by work? You who are

burdened and isolated by the trials and the responsibilities of life? You may lack all things, but not Jesus on the Cross. He is with you. He is with you.

And more, he is for us! Why the agony and death of Jesus? Let us reflect! It is the great mystery of the Cross: Jesus suffers for us! He pays a price for us. He is victim. He shares the physical evils of man to cure him from moral evil, to cancel in himself our sins.

People without hope! People who only delude yourselves, trying to reacquire peace for your consciences, which are suffocating in the depths of your inextinguishable remorse (all of us sinners are so, we must be so if we are truly human), why turn your backs on the Cross? We have the courage to turn back to it, to recognize in it our guilt. We have the confidence to sustain the sight of its mysterious figure. It speaks of mercy. It speaks of love, of resurrection. It irradiates salvation for us.

GOOD FRIDAY, APRIL 9, 1971

My beloved Redeemer, to the Cross I bring my burden of sin and fragility. Your bowed head, your wounds, your arms opened to embrace me, speak of your limitless love. At the foot of your Cross I learn mercy, compassion, forgiveness, and the price of my redemption. May I live gratefully by extending all that you teach me here to others. Loving Jesus, draw me always closer to you!

EVANGELIZATION

"Modern man listens more willingly to witnesses than to teachers, and if he does listen to teachers, it is because they are witnesses."

We Have Good News!

"Very truly, I tell you, we speak of what we know and testify to what we have seen. . . . For God so loved the world that he gave his only Son, so that everyone who believes in him may not perish but may have eternal life."

Jn 3:11,16

We are to preach the Gospel in this extraordinary period of human history, a time surely without precedent. In this time, peaks of achievement never before attained are matched by similarly unprecedented depths of bewilderment and despair. If there were ever a time when Christians were challenged to be, more than ever before, a light to illumine the world, a city on a hill, a salt to give savor to men's lives (see Mt 5:13–14), surely that time is now! For we possess the antidote to pessimism, the gloomy foreboding, the dejection and fear, which afflict our time.

We have Good News!

And every one of us, by the very nature of Christianity, must feel ourselves impelled to broadcast this Good News to the ends of the earth. "We cannot keep from speaking about what we have seen and heard" (Acts 4:20).

Not one of us Christians—pope, bishop, priest, religious, or lay person—can disclaim responsibility in regard to this essential Christian duty. . . . "Every disciple of Christ (without exception) has the obligation to do his part in spreading the faith" (*Ad Gentes*, 23). . . .

Let us be very clear on one point: Christ gave his apostles a command that is so concrete and so explicit it excludes any possibility of uncertainty about his wishes. They were to go to the whole world (without exclusion of any part) and preach the Good News to every creature (with no exception of race or time).

The Good News is this: that God loves us; that he became man to share in our life and to share his life with us; that he walks with us—every step of the way—taking our concerns as his own, for he cares about us (and that therefore no one is alone, for God is present in their entire history, that of peoples and that of individuals); that he will bring us, if we allow him, to an eternal happiness beyond the bounds of human existence (see 1 Pt 5:7).

MESSAGE FOR MISSION SUNDAY, JUNE 25, 1971

Your love for us, Heavenly Father, revealed in your Son and in the mystery of redemption, is such a source of joy and comfort! You are constantly with us, always at our side. Let this conviction take over my life more and more and make of me a convincing Christian witness and evangelizer to all those I come in contact with.

God's Great Plan

Jesus came and said to them, "All authority in heaven and
on earth has been given to me. Go therefore and make disciples of all nations, baptizing them in the name of the
Father and of the Son and of the Holy Spirit, and teaching
them to obey everything that I have commanded you. And
remember, I am with you always, to the end of the age."

Mt 28:18–20

Brothers and sisters, our stupendous and dramatic lot is
that of being involved in a wonderful divine plan, which
wishes us not only to be admitted and to be sharers in the
kingdom of God, but also to bear witness to it and spread it.
The Gospel is not a proclamation that is extinguished or stag-
nant in the one whom receives it, but a voice that resounds
and becomes an echo, a voice in its turn, a cry! Jesus taught us:
"What I say to you in the dark, tell in the light; and what you
hear whispered, proclaim from the housetops" (Mt 10:27). It
is not an episode; it is a program, which spreads through the
earth and becomes history. Christ sums up and concludes his
preaching to the Apostles as follows: "Go therefore and make
disciples of all nations" (Mt 28:19). Living faith is a faith that
spreads. The believing Church is mother and teacher, and
with the doctrine of the Council she strengthens us and warns
us that those of us who are her sons must be proud of the

Christian name, and witnesses to what this name signifies and teaches us (*Lumen Gentium*, 33). . . .

To evangelize it is necessary to be courageous, not to be afraid of anything or anyone (see Mt 10:28). This does not mean being irresponsible and rash . . . , but humble and strong, bold and sincere with everyone. And it means remembering that even disasters and difficulties can help the cause of the Gospel, our own and that of those whose welfare we wish to promote. A well-known expression of Saint Paul goes, "We know that all things work together for good for those who love God, who are called according to his purpose" (Rom 8:28). And we must renew our trust in the communion of saints, especially in the protection of the Blessed Virgin. In this way let the inventive and operative genius of human advancement, which springs from the Gospel and from this heavenly assistance, find in Christian trust, not elsewhere, that energetic conviction that makes it effective.

Message to the Pontifical Academy of Science, September 31, 1976

Bless your Church, Lord, in her task of evangelization and help me to be aware of my own responsibility of living your Gospel courageously and to proclaim it boldly. I trust that you will inspire me in every moment, and I take courage in your promise: "Proclaim the Good News to all creation; I am with you always."

Epiphany Proclamation

After Jesus was born in Bethlehem of Judea, wise men from the East came to Jerusalem, asking, "Where is the child who has been born king of the Jews? For we observed his star at its rising, and have come to pay him homage. . . . The star that they had seen at its rising, [went ahead of them] until it stopped over the place where the child was. When they saw that the star had stopped, they were overwhelmed with joy. On entering the house, they saw the child with Mary his mother; and they knelt down and paid him homage."

MT 2:1–2, 9–11

In the immense panorama of Epiphany . . . is the design of spreading the revelation that took place in Christ the Lord. Jesus came in silence and humility, but not to hide, not to set limits to the irradiation of his presence in the world. Rather [he came] to make the simpler paths accessible to those who seek him, to those who welcome him.

There is a missionary intention in the very ways in which Jesus entered the world and then carried out his evangelical plan. There is a historic-human economy, certainly directed by divine leadership, regarding the spread of the Gospel in the world. The very presence of the Wise Men in Bethlehem indicates that Jesus, as soon as he is born, is at once available for some people, [as a sign that he is] for everyone; according to a particular economy, which seems to reserve the first places for those farthest away.

With the birth of Jesus in the world a star was lit, a luminous vocation was lit. Caravans of peoples set out (see Is 60:1ff). New ways are marked out on the earth; ways that arrive, and therefore ways that depart. Christ is the center. In fact, Christ is the heart. A new circulation has begun for humanity; it will never end. On the contrary, it is destined to constitute an essential program for the Church, that is, for the community of believers in Christ which will form a body with him. It is a program, a necessity, an urgency, a continual effort, which has its *raison d'être* in the fact that Christ is the Savior. Christ is necessary. Christ is potentially universal. Christ wishes to be announced, preached, spread by a ministry of brothers and sisters, by an apostolate of men and women sent specially by him to bring to humanity the message of truth, brotherhood, freedom, and peace.

HOMILY, JANUARY 6, 1973

Jesus Incarnate, let me be like the star that by its glow leads others to you. May I always witness to you by what I think and say and do. In whatever ways I can, I want to spread your Good News to as many persons as possible, for you alone give meaning to our lives. May everyone know you, love you, and follow you, Lord.

Now Is the Time

How are they to call on one in whom they have not believed? And how are they to believe in one of whom they have never heard? And how are they to hear without someone to proclaim him? And how are they to proclaim him unless they are sent? As it is written, "How beautiful are the feet of those who bring good news!" . . . Faith comes from what is heard, and what is heard comes through the word of Christ.

Rom 10:14–17

The work of evangelization, besides being necessary, is urgent; first of all, because of divine charity, which is the supreme reason which motivates it, and then also as a reply to the great spiritual need of the present-day world. "The love of Christ urges us on" (2 Cor 5:14). From the time that Saint Paul expressed that precept, the religious panorama in the world presents characteristics that worry and sadden us. The growth of the missionary activity of the Church is too slow. It is customary to excuse this by saying that the Church should imitate the patience of God. This is true: God is patient because he is eternal. God has his hour, nor can we in our anxiety profess to advance God's hour. We do, however, forget that it is we, with our guilty selfishness, our indolence and lack of missionary zeal, who, so to speak, force God to show himself patient, almost as if maintaining the pace that we ourselves wish to keep.

God is love, and, as such, he earnestly wishes to communicate with people. Didn't these words flow from the heart of Christ, burning like volcanic lava: "I came to bring fire to the earth, and how I wish it were already kindled!" (Lk 12:49). Similarly, today's world, by the signs of our times, turns to the Church to hasten to its aid and to respond fully to its increasing disquiet and aspirations, like the Macedonian of Saint Paul's vision: "Come over to Macedonia and help us" (Acts 16:9–10). Those of us who are sons and daughters of the Church can and must reply as did the Apostle of the Gentiles: "If I proclaim the gospel, this gives me no ground for boasting, for an obligation is laid on me, and woe to me if I do not proclaim the gospel!" (1 Cor 9:16)

WORLD MISSION DAY ADDRESS, JUNE 29, 1974

Lord God, set my heart ablaze with a desire to live my faith fully and to share it freely with others. Help me to be committed to the building of your kingdom, moved by the plight of the poor, those who suffer, and those who do not know you. Grant me the heart of an apostle. Inspire many others with the desire to make you known and loved.

Selected Prayers

Attributed to Pope Saint Paul VI

Make Us Worthy, Lord

Make us worthy, Lord,
to serve our fellow men
throughout the world,
who live and die in poverty and hunger.
Give them today, through our hands,
their daily bread,
and through our understanding love,
give peace and joy. Amen.

Abandonment in God

Remember, Lord, that I am your creature.
Remember that you called me into life.
And here I am, the work of your hands,
misshapen clay, made in your image.
I am fragile in your powerful hands,
but those hands are compassionate;
they are compassionate
even when they weigh heavy upon us.
Your hands support and sustain;
your hands chastise and restore.
I will abandon my life to them;
the gift you have given me
I entrust to you.
Where nothing goes lost,

I will lose my being—
in you, Lord,
my beginning and my end. Amen.

A Prayer for Faith

[Etched in bronze on the back door of Saint Peter's Basilica]

Lord, I believe. I want to believe in you.

O Lord, make my faith pure.

O Lord, make my faith free.

O Lord, make my faith sure.

O Lord, make my faith strong.

O Lord, make my faith cheerful.

O Lord, make my faith fruitful in good works.

O Lord, make my faith humble. Amen.

Prayer for Peace

Lord, God of peace,
you created the human person,
as the object of your goodness,
to be the family of your glory;
we bless you and give you thanks.
You sent us Jesus,
your beloved Son,
and made him the source of all peace.
We give you thanks

for the desires, efforts, and achievements
that your Spirit of peace
has aroused in our time.
Open our hearts even more
to the needs and the love
of all our brothers and sisters,
so that more and more
we can be builders of peace.
Remember; Father of mercy,
all those who are in pain,
who suffer and die
giving birth to a fraternal world.
May your kingdom
of justice, peace, and love,
come for people of every language and race. Amen.

Come, Holy Spirit

Come, Holy Spirit,
and give us a new heart.
May it renew in everyone
the gifts received from you
and the joy of being Christians.
Let it be a new heart
that is always young and joyful.
Come, Holy Spirit,
and give us a pure heart,

striving to love Christ the Lord,
who is God with you
and with the Father.
Let it be a heart that does not know evil
except to define it and put it to flight.
Let it be like the heart of a child,
capable of enthusiasm and wonder.
Come, Holy Spirit,
and give us a big heart,
a heart open to your silent
and powerful word,
but closed to every mean ambition,
a stranger to every kind of rivalry.
Grant us a big heart like that of Jesus,
wide enough to contain within itself
the Church and the world.
Grant us a great and strong heart
to love all, to serve all, to suffer for all.

Lord, I Believe

Lord, I believe,
and I want to believe in you.
Lord, let my faith be full and without limits.
Let it penetrate my thoughts,
and affect how I make decisions.
Lord, let my faith be free.

Let me live it,
accepting the renunciations and duties involved,
and let it express the best of my personality.
I believe in You, Lord!
Lord, let my faith be sure:
sure of external evidence in harmony with it,
and of the interior action of the Holy Spirit;
sure of his reassuring light,
peaceful development, and
quiet assimilation.
Lord, let my faith be strong.
Let it not fear the difficulties of problems,
that we experience in our search for light.
Let it not fear the hostility of those who question it,
attack it, reject it, deny it;
but, let it be strengthened in the trusted proof of
     your truth.
Resisting the attacks of criticism,
let it be strengthened in continual affirmation,
surmounting the dialectical and spiritual difficulties
of our temporal existence.
Lord, let my faith be joyful,
and give peace and happiness to my spirit.
Let it lead me to prayer with God
and conversation with others,
so that the inner joy I have in faith
may shine forth in both holy and daily words.

Lord, let my faith be fruitful in good works,
investing my love with motivation,
that it may be true friendship with you
and reflect you in works, sufferings,
and in the expectation of the final beatitude.
Let me be tireless in my search,
constant in witnessing,
and continually nourish my hope in you.
Lord, let my faith be humble
and not believe that it comes just from
my own experiences, thoughts, or feelings.
But let my faith give itself to the Holy Spirit,
and not have any more certainty than that which comes
from obeying Tradition and the teachings of your Holy
Church. Amen.

Prayer to Mary, Our Mother

O Mary,
look upon all people,
and on this world in which
God calls us to live and work today.
Our world has turned its back
on the light of Christ;
but, then fears and cries out against
the frightening shadows that it has created.
O most beautiful Virgin, most worthy Mother,

may your voice invite the world to turn its
eyes to the life that is the light of all.
O blessed among women, may the world
turn toward you, the first lamp of Christ,
who is the only and the highest light of the world.
Show yourself a mother to us;
this is our prayer,
O clement, O loving,
O sweet Virgin Mary! Amen.

A Priest's Prayer to Mary

O Mary,
look upon us who are your children,
who are brothers and sisters,
disciples and apostles, continuing the mission of Jesus.
Make us aware of our vocation and our mission.
May we be worthy to represent Christ
and be his presence
in our priesthood,
in our words,
and in giving our lives for the faithful people
he has placed in our care.
O you who are full of grace,
may the priesthood that honors you
also be holy and immaculate.

Prayer for Vocations

O Jesus, divine shepherd of souls, you called the Apostles to be fishers of men. Move now the ardent and generous hearts of our youth and make them your followers and ministers. Let them share your thirst of universal redemption for which you renew your sacrifice on the altar every day. Lord Jesus, always interceding for us, extend our vision to the entire world where so many brothers and sisters silently pray for the light and warmth of love. By answering your call, may many generous souls continue your mission on earth; build your Mystical Body, the Church; and become the salt of the earth and the light of the world. Extend, O Lord, your loving call to many pure and generous young men and women, that they may grow in their desire for evangelical perfection and may dedicate themselves to the service of the Church and those who desperately need their assistance and love. O Lord, we pray that those who are being called and are facing obstacles in answering the call may persevere in their commitment. Amen.

Blessed Are We

We believe, O Lord, in your word. We will try to follow and live it.

Now we hear its echo reverberating in the souls of the people of our century. It seems to tell us this:

Blessed are we, if in poverty of spirit we learn to free

ourselves from false confidence in material things and to place our chief desires in spiritual and religious goods while treating the poor with respect and love, as brothers and living images of Christ.

Blessed are we, if, having acquired the meekness of the strong, we learn to renounce the deadly power of hate and vengeance, and have the wisdom to exalt above the fear of armed force the generosity of forgiveness, alliance in freedom and work, and conquest through goodness and peace.

Blessed are we, if we do not make egoism the guiding criterion of our life, nor pleasure its purpose, but learn rather to discover in sobriety our strength, in pain a source of redemption, in sacrifice the very summit of greatness.

Blessed are we, if we prefer to be the oppressed rather than the oppressors, and constantly hunger for the progress of justice.

Blessed are we, if for the kingdom of God in time and beyond time we learn to pardon and to persevere, to work and to serve, to suffer and to love.

We shall never be deceived.

BOOKS & MEDIA

A mission of the Daughters of St. Paul

As apostles of Jesus Christ, evangelizing today's world:

We are CALLED to holiness
by God's living Word and Eucharist.

We COMMUNICATE the Gospel message
through our lives and through all
available forms of media.

We SERVE the Church
by responding to the hopes and needs
of all people with the Word of God,
in the spirit of St. Paul.

For more information visit www.pauline.org.

BOOKS & MEDIA

The Daughters of St. Paul operate book and media centers at the following addresses. Visit, call, or write the one nearest you today, or find us at www.paulinestore.org.

CALIFORNIA

| 3908 Sepulveda Blvd, Culver City, CA 90230 | 310-397-8676 |
| 3250 Middlefield Road, Menlo Park, CA 94025 | 650-562-7060 |

FLORIDA

| 145 S.W. 107th Avenue, Miami, FL 33174 | 305-559-6715 |

HAWAII

| 1143 Bishop Street, Honolulu, HI 96813 | 808-521-2731 |

ILLINOIS

| 172 North Michigan Avenue, Chicago, IL 60601 | 312-346-4228 |

LOUISIANA

| 4403 Veterans Memorial Blvd, Metairie, LA 70006 | 504-887-7631 |

MASSACHUSETTS

| 885 Providence Hwy, Dedham, MA 02026 | 781-326-5385 |

MISSOURI

| 9804 Watson Road, St. Louis, MO 63126 | 314-965-3512 |

NEW YORK

| 115 E. 29th Street, New York City, NY 10016 | 212-754-1110 |

SOUTH CAROLINA

| 243 King Street, Charleston, SC 29401 | 843-577-0175 |

TEXAS

No book center; for parish exhibits or outreach evangelization, contact: 210-569-0500, or SanAntonio@paulinemedia.com, or P.O. Box 761416, San Antonio, TX 78245

VIRGINIA

| 1025 King Street, Alexandria, VA 22314 | 703-549-3806 |

CANADA

| 3022 Dufferin Street, Toronto, ON M6B 3T5 | 416-781-9131 |